CHILDREN'S AUTHORS
AND ILLUSTRATORS

CHILDREN'S AUTHORS AND ILLUSTRATORS

A Guide to Manuscript Collections in United States Research Libraries

COMPILED BY JAMES H. FRASER
WITH THE ASSISTANCE OF RENÉE I. WEBER

Phaedrus Bibliographic Series No. 1

K. G. SAUR
New York · München · London · Paris

K. G. Saur Publishing Inc.
175 Fifth Avenue
New York, N. Y. 10010
USA
Tel. (212) 477-2500
Telex 0023/238386 kgspur

K. G. Saur Verlag KG
Püssenbacherstr. 2 b
Postfach 71 10 09
D-8000 München 71
Federal Republic of Germany
Tel. (089) 798901
Telex 5212067 saur d

Clive Bingley Ltd. &
K. G. Saur Ltd.
Commonwealth House
1-19 New Oxford Street
London WC1A INE
Great Britain
Tel. (01) 404 48 18
Telex 24902 bingle g

K. G. Saur Editeur S.A.R.L.
38, rue de Bassano
F-75008 Paris
France
Tel. (01) 72355-18
Telex Iso Bur. 6 30 144

Library of Congress Cataloging in Publication Data

Fraser, James Howard, 1934-
  Children's authors and illustrators ; a guide to
manuscript collections in United States Research
libraries.

  (Phaedrus bibliographic series ; no. 1)
  Includes index.
  1. Authors--Manuscripts--Union lists.
2. Illustrators--Manuscripts--Union lists.
3. Children's literature--Manuscripts--Union lists.
4. Catalogs, Union--United States. I. Weber,
Renée I., joint author. II. Title. III. Series.
Z6611.L7F73   (PN1009.A1)   028.52   79-24990
ISBN 0-89664-950-4

Copyright © 1980 by Phaedrus, Inc.

ISBN 0-89664-950-4

Cover and title page design by John Anderson

Printed and bound in the United States of America by Braun-
Brumfield, Inc.

CONTENTS

INTRODUCTION

For a number of years I maintained a personal file on children's author and illustrator manuscript collections I encountered in reading the NATIONAL UNION CATALOG OF MANUSCRIPT COLLECTIONS. In time I incorporated information on collections from institutional guides, national subject guides and correspondence with institutions. Ultimately I thought my growing and rather tatty looking sheaf of collection notes might be incorporated into a revised edition of Carolyn Field's SUBJECT COLLECTIONS IN CHILDREN'S LITERATURE (1968). From the standpoint of periodic maintenance, a separate guide to manuscript collections with supplements now seems more to the point.

This modest beginning is presented here in hope that it will in time grow into a national union catalog of manuscript collections in children's and youth literature. To be sure, such an ambitious dream requires the participation of those who acquire this book and report the hitherto unreported collections and correct our often incomplete entries.

In this guide you will find a certain aggravating unevenness. Some of the collections are described in great detail, and for them you will know what to expect when arriving in Eugene, Oregon; Emporia, Kansas; Philadelphia, Pennsylvania; and other cities. Some entries are a bit thin and tantalizingly vague; but we reported what was reported to us or to those general guides which also attempted to elicit a useful description of a given collection. Whatever the quantity of information, we have listed under the entry heading, in alphabetical sequence by institution, at least a clue for the researcher and a suggestion that in a particular location some material of use may be found. A directory of the institutions cited is included at the end of the text so that the researcher may contact the institution for further information.

It is our hope that those curators who discover little data regarding their own collections will be moved to report fuller information with a renewed interest in their holdings. (Our first supplement will contain augmentations to cited collections in addition to new collections.) Our hope is that all collections will at some future time be described in the manner in which those of the Free Library of Philadelphia, the University of Oregon, etc. have been described. The monumental Kerlan Collection (University of Minnesota) we hope will some day provide the public with a complete guide or provide us with material which can be incorporated in more detailed form here. Asterisks by entries in the main body indicate Kerlan Collection holdings for these individuals. A table of authors and illustrators represented in the Kerlan Collection is included following the title index.

A word about terminology. In our descriptions we have used the phrase "miscellaneous papers" to designate those holdings which do not appear to be the principle body of papers produced by an author or illustrator. The phrase "papers" indicates that as nearly as can be determined, the collection so-designated contains the nucleus of the author's or illustrator's correspondence, manuscripts etc. or the largest part of the surviving papers. "Manuscripts" are just that, the holograph or typescript work intended ultimately for a waiting printer. "Original art" is used to designate the artist's original graphic production, and may range from finished work to doodles.

We have taken the liberty of modifying descriptions which have appeared in the NATIONAL UNION CATALOG OF MANUSCRIPT COLLECTIONS in order to conform to our pattern of description. In this case the information remains the same but appears in modified form. In the case of NUCMU entries for some institutions, we have changed the phrase "papers" to "miscellaneours papers" if it appears that what is held by the reporting institution is no more than a miscellaneous accumulation and does not represent the major portion of the author's or illustrator's life record of correspondence or any major portion thereof.

As to the bibliographical side of the entries: where the material centers on a given production, we have so indicated and provided the title of the book but not the author or the illustrator. The title remains the point of access and we have provided a title index where one may find the author's name if the illustrator and author are two individuals. The dates provided for the titles are those of the first printing. Sometimes they are at odds with what has been reported to us. We have used the CUMULATIVE BOOK INDEX, the NATIONAL UNION CATALOG, and the LIBRARY OF CONGRESS CATALOG as well as other author bibliographies for verification.

The inclusion of authors or illustrators working primarily for an adult audience - Defoe, Dickens, R. H. Davis, etc. - depends upon child and adolescent appropriation of the work of these individuals.

A group of papers may seem to have little to do with the writer's concern for children and young people, and that focus is not implied by inclusion. What is implied is that whatever the content of the papers, there may be some bearing on the lives of the authors and illustrators and that this is important potentially to those who might make inquiry.

A word about interpreting certain not so obvious matters of
organization within the entry: those entries in capital letters
which are flush with the left margin of the text are considered
subordinate to the main entry and are included because of
important materials associated with the author. The symbols
(A), (I), (A,I) following the dates of the person indicate:
(A) author; (I) illustrator and (A,I) author, illustrator.
For those institutions where only the name of the holding
university is cited, the user should assume that the collection
is in the main library and for the complete address should
consult the directory of institutions at the back of this
volume. For purposes of saving space we did not use the
memorial name of a given library unless it was necessary to
avoid confusion with other campus libraries. Memorial names
appear in the institutional directory.

We have used conventional abbreviations throughout except for
the post office abbreviations of states. Here we have
perpetuated the more understandable traditional abbreviations
rather than confuse our domestic and foreign users with the
newly inaugurated code.

Information on copying and literary rights can be obtained by
writing to the collection curator; however, we have found that
in all but a few, copying is permitted provided the condition
of the material permit such.

We wish to thank those curators who have assisted in the
provision of information and the editors of the NATIONAL UNION
CATALOG OF MANUSCRIPT COLLECTIONS for permission to cite
entries from the various volumes.

James H. Fraser

COLLECTIONS

ABBOTT, JACOB, 1803-1877 (A)
  papers. "several thousand items"
  In Bowdoin College Library (Brunswick, Me.)
  Mss. and correspondence relating to eighty-five of J. Abbott's
  books.

ABBOTT, JOHN STEVENS CABOT, 1805-1877 (A)
  misc. papers. 95 items
  In Univ. of Michigan, William L. Clements Library (Ann Arbor,
  Mich.)
  Correspondence addressed to Abbott, including autograph album,
  1851-60.

ADAMS, ADRIENNE (I)
  original art. 58 items
  In Emporia State Univ. Library, May Massee Collection
  (Emporia, Kan.)
  Misc. artwork for: THE BOY JONES (1943), THE FAIRY DOLL
  (1956), THE STORY OF HOLLY AND IVY (1958), CANDY FLOSS (1960).

ADSHEAD, GLADYS LUCY, 1896-   (A)
  papers, 1939-61. ca. 2 ft.
  In Univ. of Oregon Library (Eugene, Or.)
  Includes mss. of or related material for eight books.

ALCOTT, LOUISA MAY, 1832-1888 (A)
  misc. papers, ca. 1848-85. 76 items and 3 reels of microfilm
  (negative and positive)
  In Concord Free Public Library (Concord, Mass.)
  In part, microfilm made in 1957 from originals in Houghton
  Library, Harvard Univ. Personal and family correspondence
  relating to Miss Alcott's European travels with her sister
  May in 1870; fairy tales written as a teenager for Ellen
  Emerson, daughter of Ralph Waldo Emerson; manuscript chapters
  and fragments of Thoreau's FLUTE (1862), verse written upon
  the death of Henry David Thoreau; LITTLE WOMEN (1868), LITTLE
  MEN (1871) and JACK AND JILL (1880); and 64 drawings for
  LITTLE WOMEN by Frank Merrill, annotated by Miss Alcott.
  Correspondents include William Torrey Harris, Alfred Hosmer,
  and Jean M. Lebrun.

  misc. papers.
  In Harvard Univ., Houghton Library (Cambridge, Mass.)

  papers, 1856-1918. ca. 2 ft. 311 items
  In Univ. of Virginia Library, Clifton Waller Barrett
  Collection (Charlottesville, Va.)
  Correspondence, literary mss., legal documents, book reviews,
  obituaries, and photos, relating to Miss Alcott's literary
  career, publication of her works, her family, friends,

3

ALCOTT, LOUISA MAY
  financial affairs, health, social life, the Concord School of
  Philosophy, and her sister, artist May Alcott. Correspondents
  include Lydia Maria (Francis) Child, Lydia (Dodge) Cabot
  Parker, and Elizabeth Palmer Peabody. Includes drafts for
  short stories and pages from some of her books, legal papers
  pertaining to her will and estate.

ALCOTT, AMOS BRONSON, 1799-1888
  papers, 1814-1902. 3 ft. (87 items) and 41 reels of
  microfilm (negative and positive)
  In Concord Free Public Library (Concord, Mass.)
  In part, microfilm made in 1956-57 from originals in Houghton
  Library, Harvard Univ.
  Correspondence, journals and diaries (1826-82), lectures,
  poems, and other writings; 12 scrapbooks (1879-88), containing
  programs, lectures, meeting records, faculty and student
  lists, and other papers of the Concord School of Philosophy;
  and 6 Concord town reports (1859-65), containing reports by
  Alcott as public school superintendent. Includes
  correspondence (1873-1902) between William T. Harris and
  Franklin Benjamin Sanborn, relating to Alcott; letters of
  Louisa May Alcott and other members of the family; and
  material on the philosophy of education, Goethe, and the
  antislavery movement and John Brown.

ALCOTT FAMILY
  papers, 1845-1915, 1929-32. ca. 130 items
  In Univ. of Virginia Library, Clifton Waller Barrett
  Collection (Charlottesville, Va.)
  Correspondence (1845-1915) of members of the Amos Bronson
  Alcott family; newspaper and play (ca. 1845) written by the
  Alcott children; 3 scrapbooks kept by Abigail (May) Alcott,
  and clippings. Includes letters of Abigail (May) Alcott,
  concerning financial difficulties; correspondence relating to
  the publication of Louisa May Alcott's LITTLE WOMEN (1868),
  the administration of her estate, and the domestic lives of
  her niece and nephews, Louise May Nieriker, John Sewall Pratt
  Alcott, and Frederic Alcott Pratt; and 20 letters (1904-06)
  between John Sewall Pratt Alcott and Jessie (Bonstelle)
  Stuart concerning a dramatic adaptation of LITTLE WOMEN.
  Other correspondents include Samuel Joseph May, Abigail May
  (Alcott) Nieriker, Louisa May Nieriker, Anna Bronson (Alcott)
  Pratt, Roberts Brothers (publishers), and Franklin Benjamin
  Sanborn.

MAY FAMILY
  May-Goddard family papers, 1766-1904. 2 boxes and 2 v.
  In Radcliffe College, Women's Archives (Cambridge, Mass.)
  Correspondence, diaries, documents, account books, photos,

MAY FAMILY
and memorabilia of the May and Goddard families of New
England. Persons represented include Louisa May Alcott,
Ednah Dow Cheney, Julia Ward Howe, Frederick Warren Goddard
May (1821-1904), Samuel May (1810-1899), Samuel J. May
(1797-1871), Elizabeth Stuart Phelps, and Lucy Stone.

ALDRICH, THOMAS BAILEY, 1836-1907 (A)
  misc. papers.
  In Harvard Univ., Widener Library (Cambridge, Mass.)
  For a description of this collection see HARVARD ALUMNI
  BULLETIN. 21: 852-54 (1920).

  misc. papers, 1855-1906. 118 items
  In Henry E. Huntington Library (San Marino, Calif.)
  Mss. of literary works and letters to James T. Fields and
  others.

  misc. papers
  In Princeton Univ. Library (Princeton, N.J.)

  misc. papers, 1856-1911. ca. 150 items
  In Univ. of Virginia Library, Clifton Waller Barrett
  Collection (Charlottesville, Va.)
  Correspondence, chiefly relating to Aldrich's editorship of
  the ATLANTIC MONTHLY (1881-90) and attempts to publish his
  own works, 27 manuscript poems, engravings, and photos.
  Correspondents include Madison Julius Cawein, Richard Watson
  Gilder, Thomas Wentworth Higginson, Robert Underwood Johnson,
  Edmund Clarence Stedman, and William Winter.

ALGER, HORATIO, 1832-1899 (A)
  misc. papers
  In Harvard Univ., Widener Library (Cambridge, Mass.)

  misc. papers, 1870-98. 88 items
  In Henry E. Huntington Library (San Marino, Calif.)
  Letters to Irving Blake and others.

SELIGMAN FAMILY
  misc. papers, 1877-1934. 190 items
  In American Jewish Archives (Cincinnati, Ohio)
  In part, photocopies. Correspondence relating to family
  affairs, business matters, and contemporary events, of a New
  York City family. Includes correspondence between Edwin R. A.
  Seligman and Horatio Alger, Jr., regarding Ulysses S. Grant,
  Brigham Young, the campaign of 1876, Rutherford B. Hayes and
  Alger's novels; and love letters from "Stella," niece of Edwin
  Seligman's brother. Other correspondents include Emma
  Westermann and Carrie Wise.

ALLEN, DON B., 1899-1969 (A)
   papers of Don B. Allen and Thelma Diener Allen, 1951-1967.
   4.5 ft.
   In Univ. of Oregon Library (Eugene, Or.)
   Papers include mss. of books and screenplays. Correspondence
   is with editors and publishers. Major correspondents are
   Harper and Bros., University of Oklahoma Press, Fawcett
   Publications.

AMERICAN SUNDAY-SCHOOL UNION
   records, 1817-1932. ca. 135 ft. 800,000 items
   In Presbyterian Historical Society (Philadelphia, Pa.)
   Correspondence, including letters from missionaries to the
   Indians and Negroes, in frontier areas, and in foreign lands;
   missionary reports and maps of frontier areas, general and
   financial histories of the union; printed catalogs
   (1822-1916); and copyright documents. Includes records
   (1817-1824) of the Union's predecessor, the Philadelphia
   Sunday and Adult School Union. Persons represented include
   Joseph Bruce Adams, Albert Barnes, Henry Ward Beecher,
   Lyman Beecher, George Duffield, John W. Dulles, Joseph Heatly
   Dulles, Theodore Frelinghuysen, David Gage, Charles Hodge,
   Thomas Janeway, John C. Lowrie, Walter Lowrie, William
   Augustus Muhlenberg, Frederick A. Packard, Edwin Wilbur Rice,
   S. S. Schmucker, William C. Thomson, William Torrey,
   Schuyler Van Renssaleer, John Wanamaker, Bushrod Washington,
   S. Wells Williams, and John Witherspoon.

ANDERSEN, HANS CHRISTIAN, 1805-1875 (A)
   misc. collection of Andersen book mss.
   In Indiana Univ., Lilly Library (Bloomington, Ind.)

   misc. papers. ca. 140 items
   In Library of Congress, Rare Books Division, (Washington,
   D. C.)
   Forms part of the Jean Hersholt collection of Hans Christian
   Andersen. Letters, an autobiography, and miscellaneous mss.
   Correspondents include Richard Bentley, Ida Koch, Horace E.
   Scudder, and Henrietta Wulff. Described in CATALOG OF THE
   JEAN HERSHOLT COLLECTION OF HANS CHRISTIAN ANDERSEN.
   Washington, D. C.: Library of Congress, 1954.

ANDERSON, CLARENCE WILLIAM, 1891-1971 (I)*
   original art. 4 items
   In Univ. of Oregon Library (Eugene, Or.)
   Misc. artwork for: BLAZE AND THE GRAY SPOTTED PONY (1968).

ANGELI, MARGUERITE DE (A,I)
   original art. 1 item
   In Emporia State Univ. Library, May Massee Collection

ANGELI, MARGUERITE DE
(Emporia, Kan.)
Misc. artwork for: MEGGY MACINTOSH (1944).

ANGELO, VALENTI, 1897-   (A,I)*
original art. 66 items
In Emporia State Univ. Library, May Massee Collection
(Emporia, Kan.)
Misc. artwork for: ROLLER SKATES (1936), NINO (1938), THE
LONG CHRISTMAS (1941).

ANNIXTER, PAUL and ANNIXTER, JANE LEVINGTON
pseuds. see STURTZEL, HOWARD ALLISON

APPEL, BENJAMIN, 1907-   (A)
misc. papers, 1932-1966. 5 ft.
In Univ. of Oregon Library (Eugene, Or.)
Papers include mss. of books, galley and page proofs, copies
of published books and articles, and minor correspondence.

ARCHER, JULES, 1915-   (A)
papers, 1952-78. ca. 17 ft.
In Univ. of Oregon Library (Eugene, Or.)
Correspondence with agent and editors, mss. of four
biographies.

ARCHIBALD, JOSEPH STOPFORD, 1898-   (A)
misc. papers. 2 folders
In Univ. of Oregon Library (Eugene, Or.)

ARNTSON, HERBERT EDWARD, 1911-   (A)
misc. papers, 1957-76. 7 ft.
In Univ. of Oregon Library (Eugene, Or.)
Mss. include drafts, notes, and successive versions of many
books.

ARTZYBASHEFF, BORIS, 1899-1965 (A,I)*
original art. 13 items
In Emporia State Univ. Library, May Massee Collection
(Emporia, Kan.)
Misc. artwork for: SEVEN SIMEONS (1937)

papers
In Columbia Univ., Butler Library (N. Y.)

ASIMOV, ISAAC, 1920-   (A)
papers, 1949-64. 8 ft.
In Boston Univ. Library (Boston, Mass.)
Business correspondence with publishers; letters from
scientists about his work; typescripts and carbons of his

ASIMOV, ISAAC
  works of science and science fiction.
  Additions to the collection are anticipated.

ATWATER, MONTGOMERY MEIGS, 1904-1976 (A)
  misc. papers, 1955-66. 3 ft.
  In Univ. of Oregon Library (Eugene, Or.)
  Wrote short stories and mysteries, often for children, some
  under the pseudonym of Max Montgomery. Papers include minor
  correspondence with publishers, mss. of books and articles.

AULAIRE, EDGAR PARIN, D', 1898-   (A,I)*
  original art. 31 items
  In Univ. of Oregon Library (Eugene, Or.)
  The lithographs are one of four complete sets of originals for
  the book, BUFFALO BILL (1952).

AUSTIN, MARY (HUNTER), 1868-1934 (A)
  papers, 1861-1950. ca. 11,000 items
  In Henry E. Huntington Library (San Marino, Calif.)
  Correspondence and personal and literary papers.

AYER, MARGARET (A,I)*
  misc. papers, 1944-64. 1.5 ft.
  In Univ. of Oregon Library (Eugene, Or.)
  Papers include illustrations for MADE IN THAILAND (1964) and
  for books by other authors such as Catherine Pears; the
  manuscript of Ayer's ANIMALS OF SOUTHEAST ASIA (1970), a
  correspondence file and some published material.

BABCOCK FAMILY
  papers, 1788-1869. ca. 1,200 items
  In Connecticut Historical Society (Hartford, Conn.)
  Family and business correspondence and accounts of the
  Babcock family, particularly Elisha Babcock (1735-1821), John
  Babcock (1764-1843), and Sidney Babcock (1797-1884), printers
  in Hartford and New Haven, Conn.

  BABCOCK, JOHN, 1764-1843
  John and Sidney Babcock papers, 1800-71. 134 items
  In American Antiquarian Society (Worcester, Mass.)
  Printers, of Hartford and New Haven, Conn. Correspondence,
  business records, and receipts, of Babcock and his son, Sidney
  Babcock, reflecting their business careers and the political
  interests of John Babcock.

BALCH, EMILY GREENE, 1867-1961 (A)
  papers, 1893-1948. 20 ft.
  In Swarthmore College, Friends Historical Library
  (Swarthmore, Pa.)

BALCH, EMILY GREENE
  Correspondence (on problems of minorities, boundaries, postwar
  planning, world government, and organization for peace),
  travel journal, clippings, pamphlets, and typewritten,
  mimeographed and printed articles and books by Miss Balch on
  international questions and policies of the Women's Peace
  Party, Women's Committee for Permanent Peace, and the Women's
  International League for Peace and Freedom in which she took
  active part. Correspondents include Grace Abbott, Jane Addams,
  Henry W. Longfellow Dana, Louis Lochner, and Oswald Garrison
  Villard. The material is related to the library's Jane Addams
  and Women's International League for Peace and Freedom
  collections. Described in GUIDE TO SWARTHMORE COLLEGE PEACE
  COLLECTION: A MEMORIAL TO JANE ADDAMS. Swarthmore, Pa.:
  Swarthmore College, 1947.

BARRIE, SIR JAMES, 1860-1937 (A)
  misc. papers
  In Harvard Univ., Houghton Library (Cambridge, Mass.)

  misc. papers
  In Indiana Univ., Lilly Library (Bloomington, Ind.)

  misc. papers. ca. 150 items
  In Princeton Univ. Library (Princeton, N.J.)
  PRINCETON UNIVERSITY LIBRARY CHRONICLE 17:96-98, 1956
  describes the miscellaneous "prose pieces" and correspondence
  of this collection.

  misc. papers
  In Yale Univ., Beinecke Library (New Haven, Conn.)
  Over 500 letters mostly to Lady Asquith and her family.

BAUM, LYMAN FRANK, 1856-1919 (A)
  misc. papers, 1871-1961. 320 items
  In Columbia Univ., Butler Library (N.Y.)
  Correspondence, literary mss., and other papers by and about
  Baum, chiefly relating to the centenary Baum exhibition held
  at Columbia University in 1956.

  misc. papers
  In Syracuse Univ. Library (Syracuse, N.Y.)
  "...material consists primarily of typescripts of the L. Frank
  Baum biography by Baum and McFall and of the correspondence
  between these two."

BEADLE, ERASTUS FLAVEL, 1821-1894 (printer and publisher)
  misc. papers, 1753-1922. 1 box
  In New York Public Library, Research Division (N.Y.)
  Correspondence, diary, accounts, notes and newspaper clippings,

BEADLE, ERASTUS FLAVEL
and other papers relating to Beadle, his family, and the
Beadle Publishing Company. Includes diary (1857) of Beadle's
journey from Buffalo, N.Y. to his preempted lands near Omaha,
Neb., genealogical notes of the Beadle family in Mass., Conn.,
and N.Y.; letters (1865-97) to and from Orville J. Victor,
and letters and mss. of contributors to Beadle publications
such as Henri, Comte de Baumet, George Waldo Browne,
C. Dunning Clark, Oll Coomes, Edward Sylvester Ellis, William
S. Gridley, Thomas C. Harbaugh, Horace Seymour Keller, Charles
Bertrand Lewis, Will Lisenbee, Tom P. Morgan, Washington
Whitehorn, and John H. Witson.

BEARD, DANIEL CARTER, 1850-1941 (A,I)
papers, 1798-1941. 120 ft.
In Library of Congress, Manuscript Division (Washington, D.C.)
Correspondence, diaries, speeches, articles, collected source
material for further articles and speeches, school composition
books, illustrations, photos, memorabilia, and other printed
matter relating to Beard's activities at the Culver Military
Academy, at the Dan Beard Outdoor School, and in the Boy
Scouts. Includes family papers dating from 1798 which
contain writings and illustrations by other members of the
family, and reports, minutes, circulars and publications,
letters to and from BOY'S LIFE magazine (1911-   )
and other correspondence relating to the Boy Scouts.
Correspondents include Robert Baden-Powell, Belmore Browne,
Samuel L. Clemens, Hamlin Garland, Charles Dana Gibson,
Gifford Pinchot, Frederic Remington, Franklin D. Roosevelt,
Theodore Roosevelt, Ernest T. Seton, and Andrew J. Stone.

BEATTY, HETTY BURLINGAME, 1906- (A,I)
papers, 1947-68. 8 ft.
In Univ. of Oregon Library (Eugene, Or.)
Papers consist of mss. and original artwork for 12 books, and
correspondence mainly with Houghton Mifflin Co.

BECKER, MAY (LAMBERTON), 1873-1958 (A)
misc. papers, 1921-39. 50 items
In Temple Univ. Library (Philadelphia, Pa.)
Correspondents include Louis Bromfield, James Branch Cabell,
Erskine Caldwell, James Hilton, John Masefield, A. A. Milne,
Christopher Morley, Upton Sinclair, Frank Swinnerton, and
Daniel Berkeley Updike.

BEHN, HARRY, 1898-1973 (A)*
misc. papers, 1914-68. 1.5 ft.
In Univ. of Oregon Library (Eugene, Or.)
Includes 28 screenplays, scenarios, screen treatments and
continuities written 1926-39, among them "The Big Parade,"

BEHN, HARRY
  "The Crowd," and "Hell's Angels." There are also nine play
  mss. and minor correspondence.

BELL, CORYDON (I)
  original art. 21 items
  In Emporia State Univ. Library, May Massee Collection
  (Emporia, Kan.)
  Misc. artwork for: SNOW (1954), THE MAGIC PIN (1956), THE
  SECRET CIRCLE (1958), THUNDERSTORM (1960), I WILL ADVENTURE
  (1962), THE RIDDLE OF TIME (1963).

BEMELMANS, LUDWIG, 1898-1962 (A,I)
  original art. 6 items
  In Emporia State Univ. Library, May Massee Collection
  (Emporia, Kan.)
  Misc. artwork for: HANSI (1934), THE CASTLE NUMBER NINE
  (1937), MADELINE AND THE GYPSIES (1959).

BENARY-ISBERT, MARGOT, 1889-1979 (A)*
  papers, 1950-72. 8 ft., including ca. 1,500 letters
  In Univ. of Oregon Library (Eugene, Or.)
  Includes mss. of books for children, correspondence with
  German and American publishers, and original illustrations.

BENDICK, JEANNE, 1919-   (A,I)*
  papers, 1950-75. 15 ft.
  In Univ. of Oregon Library (Eugene, Or.)
  Literary mss., galley proofs, and original illustrations for
  books by Mrs. Bendick and others.

BENET, STEPHEN VINCENT, 1898-1943 (A)
  misc. papers
  In Yale Univ., Beinecke Library (New Haven, Conn.)

BERGER, JOSEPH, 1903-1972 (A)
  misc. papers, 1938-69. ca. 2 ft.
  In Univ. of Oregon Library (Eugene, Or.)
  Mss. of 4 books, 14 published works, and interview with Berger.

BETTINA
  pseud. see EHRLICH, BETTINA

BEWICK, THOMAS, 1753-1828 (I)
  misc. papers, 1796-1828. 55 items
  In Henry E. Huntington Library (San Marino, Calif.)
  Correspondence of Bewick with his daughter, Jane, together
  with a few letters to and from other members of the family.

  original art
  In Newberry Library (Chicago, Ill.)

11

BLASSINGAME, LURTON (literary agent)
papers, 1965-75. 25 ft., including 25,000 letters
In Univ. of Oregon Library (Eugene, Or.)
Files contain correspondence to and from clients, publishers,
and editors, including royalty reports. Correspondents
include Wyatt Blassingame, Merle Constiner, Maureen Daly
(Mrs. William McGivern), Charles Einstein, Leonard Falkner,
Gertrude Elva Bridgeman Finney, Robert Fontaine, Neta L.
Frazier, Robert Anson Heinlein, Edwin Hoag, Adolf A.
Hoehling, Anne Roller Issler, James Herz Joseph, James
Kjelgaard, Robert G. Krauss, Sidney Lens, Mike McGrady, Arthur
Orrmont, Alonzo Pond, Margaret Scherf, Donald Kent Stanford,
G. Harry Stine, Marcella Thum, and Robert W. and Janet R.
Young.

BLOCKLINGER, PEGGY O'MORE, 1895-1970 (A)
papers, 1927-65. 6 ft.
In Univ. of Oregon Library (Eugene, Or.)
Includes 32 book mss., correspondence with agents and
publishers, copies of books and other published material.
Author's books published under variety of pseudonyms, most
often Peggy O'More, or Jeanne Bowman.

BLOUGH, GLENN O., 1907-   (A)*
papers. 3 ft.
In Univ. of Oregon Library (Eugene, Or.)
Collection includes mss. of author's books, plus galleys,
dummies, related correspondence and some reviews.

BOBBS-MERRILL COMPANY
papers, 1885-1957. misc. records
In Indiana Univ., Lilly Library (Bloomington, Ind.)

BOHANON, EUNICE BLAKE, 1904-   (editor)
misc. papers, 1964-66. 1 ft.
In Univ. of Oregon Library (Eugene, Or.)
Collection includes correspondence relating to her tours of
India, Pakistan, Israel, Italy and the Philippines, plus mss.
of reports and articles on her work and assorted clippings.

BONTEMPS, ARNA WENDELL, 1902-1973 (A)
papers, 1939-61. 12 ft.
In Syracuse Univ. Library (Syracuse, N.Y.)
Correspondence; mss. of various versions of Mr. Bontemp's
books, a musical, plays, reports, songs, and speeches; photos,
and published materials. Correspondents include Nelson
Algren, Countee Cullen, W. C. Handy, and Clare Booth Luce.

BOWMAN, JEANNE
pseud. see BLOCKLINGER, PEGGY O'MORE

BOYD, EDITH L. (A)
  misc. papers, 1958-60. 11 items
  In Washingon State Univ. Library (Pullman, Wash.)
  Correspondence with her agent and others; mss. of BOY JOE
  GOES TO SEA (1959).

BRANN, ESTHER (A,I)
  misc. papers, 1924-60. 1 box
  In Univ. of Oregon Library (Eugene, Or.)
  Correspondence with the Macmillan Co. and mss. of 8 books.

BRATTON, HELEN, 1899-   (A)
  misc. papers, 1962-69. ca. 2 ft.
  In Univ. of Oregon Library (Eugene, Or.)
  Correspondence mainly with David McKay Co.; literary mss.,
  including drafts and final copies.

BROOKS, ANNE TEDLOCK, 1905-   (A)
  misc. papers, 1939-50. ca. 2 ft.
  In Univ. of Oregon Library (Eugene, Or.)
  Mss. of THE SINGING FIDDLES, A STORY OF THE JASON LEE MISSIONS
  IN EARLY OREGON (1950) and FIRE IN THE WIND (1950).
  Correspondence is with agents and editors, particularly Willis
  Wing, May Cameron of Samuel Curl, Inc., and Arcadia House.

BROWN, MARGARET WISE, 1910-1952 (A,I)*
  misc. papers. original art
  In Westerly Public Library (Westerly, R.I.)
  Mss. and unpublished writings; original art for LITTLE BRASS
  BAND (1955), dummies for misc. Little Golden books. Uncataloged.

BROWN, WILLIAM LOUIS, 1910-1965 (editor)
  papers, 1935-62. 1.5 ft. including ca. 800 letters
  In Univ. of Oregon Library (Eugene, Or.)
  Papers include mss. of 2 books and 15 short stories and
  articles. Correspondence consists of letters by Brown in
  1936-37 on his South Seas voyage and his soldier's letters,
  1942-45, from Ft. Dix, N.J., and India and Burma. He was
  editor of his service group newspaper, "The Gremlin," and
  the papers include a file of that publication. Correspondents
  include Alice Torrey, editor of Coward-McCann; literary agents,
  C. V. Parkinson and McIntosh & Otis; and 6 letters from
  Stewart Holbrook. Copies of his published books are included,
  2 of them written in collaboration with his wife, Rosalie Moore
  Brown.

BULLA, CLYDE ROBERT, 1914-   (A)*
  misc. papers. 2 items
  In Univ. of Oregon Library (Eugene, Or.)
  Mss. of DEXTER (1946) and THE MOON SINGER (1969).

BURGER, CARL, 1888-1968 (A,I)*
  misc. papers, 1967-68. 3 ft.
  In Univ. of Oregon Library (Eugene, Or.)
  Collection includes 21 original drawings and 4 maps for
  BEAVER SKINS AND MOUNTAIN MEN (1968).

BURGESS, THORNTON W., 1874-1965 (A)
  misc. papers and photographs
  In Sandwich Public Library (Sandwich, Mass.)

BURROUGHS, EDGAR RICE, 1875-1950 (A)
  papers, 1911-1947. 78 storage file drawers
  In the Archives of Edgar Rice Burroughs, Inc. (Tarzana,
  Calif.)
  Including personal correspondence and business records,
  papers relating to Motion Picture and Burroughs-Tarzan
  Enterprises, Inc., ERB's correspondence with publishers,
  fan letters, scripts of Tarzan, radio serials, merchandise
  franchises.

BURROUGHS, JOHN, 1837-1921 (A)
  papers, 1904-21. ca. 200 items
  In American Academy of Arts and Letters Library (N.Y.)
  Correspondence chiefly relating to the National Institute of
  Arts and Letters, to the American Academy of Arts and Letters,
  and to various articles, trips, and projects; and two
  scrapbooks. Names prominently mentioned are Thomas Bailey
  Aldrich, Robert Underwood Johnson, and Theodore Roosevelt.

  misc. papers, 1893-1921. ca. 40 items
  In Henry E. Huntington Library (San Marino, Calif.)
  Literary mss. and letters to Francis F. Browne and others.

BURTON, VIRGINIA LEE, 1909-1968 (A,I)
  misc. papers, 1962. 476 items
  In Free Library of Philadelphia (Philadelphia, Pa.)
  Typescript and miscellaneous artwork for: LIFE STORY (1962).

  misc. papers. 2 boxes
  In Univ. of Oregon Library (Eugene, Or.)
  Collection inculudes preliminary sketches and final drawings
  for six of her books, including the first and second editions
  of CALICO, THE WONDER HORSE; OR, THE SAGA OF STEWY SLINKER
  (1941).

CALL, HUGHIE FLORENCE, 1890-1969 (A)
  misc papers. 1.5 ft.
  In Univ. of Oregon Library (Eugene, Or.)
  Collection includes correspondence, mss. of GOLDEN FLEECE
  (1942), THE LITTLE KINGDOM (1964) and THE SHORN LAMB (1969),

CALL, HUGHIE FLORENCE
  research notes, clippings and memorabilia.

CAPP, AL, 1909-   (cartoonist)
  cartoon strips, 1958-65. 1,009 items
  In Boston Univ. Library (Boston, Mass.)
  Original pen and ink drawings of the "Li'l Abner" cartoon
  strips.

CAREY, MATHEW, 1760-1839, (publisher)
  business records, 1787-1822. ca. 50,000 items
  In Historical Society of Pennsylvania (Philadelphia, Pa.)
  Letter books, chiefly containing correspondence with American
  bookdealers, Carey's correspondence with prominent political
  and literary personalities and Thomas Jefferson letters
  (1801 and 1820) commenting on schoolbooks and scientific
  publications.

CARR, MARY JANE, 1899-   (A)*
  misc. papers, 1940-58. 1 box
  In Univ. of Oregon Library (Eugene, Or.)
  Papers include a carbon manuscript of CHILDREN OF THE COVERED
  WAGON (1934) and three original illustrations by Robert Kuhn
  for the book.

CARRIGHAR, SALLY (A)
  misc. papers, 1943-66. 3 ft.
  In Boston Univ. Library (Boston, Mass.)
  Chiefly business correspondence, financial records, mss.,
  photos., drawings, clippings, and memorabilia.
  Additions to this collection are anticipated.

CARROLL, GLADYS (HASTY), 1904-   (A)
  papers, 1915-64. 9 ft.
  In Boston Univ. Library (Boston, Mass.)
  Personal and professional correspondence (1933-44) relating to
  Bates College and letters from national political figures
  relating to interest in Republican Party; 152 mss. of Mrs.
  Carroll's short stories and articles, including 15 of her
  novels and some juvenilia; clippings and other publicity
  material consisting of 8 scrapbooks and 1 carton on all of her
  works, including the motion picture and folk play versions of
  AS THE EARTH TURNS (1933).
  Additions to this collection are anticipated.

CARROLL, LEWIS
  pseud. see DODGSON, CHARLES LUTWIDGE

CARROLL, RUTH (ROBINSON), 1899-   (I)
  papers of Ruth and Latrobe Carroll, 1945-75. 12 ft.

CARROLL, RUTH (ROBINSON)
   In Univ. of Oregon Library (Eugene, Or.)
   Includes 30 letters (1965-72) from Berta Hader, literary mss.,
   artwork, and autographed presentation copies of books by
   Elmer and Berta Hader and children's books written with her
   husband, Latrobe Carroll.

CASTLE, FRANK P. (A)
   misc. papers, 1948-66. ca. 2 ft.
   In Univ. of Oregon Library (Eugene, Or.)
   Includes 120 mss. of short fiction for pulp magazines, 47 by
   Thomas W. Blackburn, and 23 comic strip scripts.

CASTOR, HENRY, 1909-   (A)
   misc. papers, 1953-70
   In Univ. of Oregon Library (Eugene, Or.)
   Collection includes mss. for 3 books, AMERICA'S FIRST WORLD
   WAR (1959), FIFTY-FOUR FORTY OR FIGHT! (1970) and TRIPOLITAN
   WAR, 1801-1805 (1971), all typed with holograph revisions,
   plus related correspondence.

CAUDILL, REBECCA (A) *
   misc. papers. 69 items
   In Emporia State Univ. Library, May Massee Collection
   (Emporia, Kan.)
   Consists of correspondence with May Massee.

CAVANAH, FRANCES, 1899-   (A)*
   misc. papers, 1968-69. 1.5 ft.
   In Univ. of Oregon Library (Eugene, Or.)
   Papers consist of book mss., correspondence with publishers.

CENTURY COMPANY
   records, ca. 1870-1917. 207 boxes
   In New York Public Library (N.Y.)
   Includes correspondence, mss., and vouchers (ca. 1911-17) of
   ST. NICHOLAS magazine.

CHARLOT, JEAN, 1898-   (I)*
   original art. 38 items
   In Emporia State Univ. Library, May Massee Collection
   (Emporia, Kan.)
   Misc. artwork for: THE CORN GROWS RIPE (1956)

CHASE, MARY COYLE, 1907-   (A)
   papers, 1947-68. 1 ft.
   In Univ. of Oregon Library (Eugene, Or.)
   Papers consist of mss. and plays, and books, writing for
   children, and minor correspondence. Among the play mss. are
   early versions and revisions of "Bernadine" and "Harvey," and
   a screen treatment of Harvey. The final manuscript of

16

CHASE, MARY COYLE
  "Harvey" is in the library of the Univ. of Denver.

CHASE, MARY ELLEN, 1887-1973 (A)
  misc. papers
  In Boston Univ. Library (Boston, Mass.)

  misc. papers, 1909-64. 3 ft.
  In Westbrook Junior College Library, Maine Women Writers'
  Collection (Portland, Me.)
  Correspondence, documents, and clippings relating to Chase's
  publications.

CHASTAIN, MADYE LEE, 1908-   (A,I)*
  misc. papers. 1 box, including 31 illustrations
  In Univ. of Oregon Library (Eugene, Or.)
  Manuscript and original illustrations for STEAMBOAT SOUTH
  (1951).

CHILD, LYDIA MARIA, 1802-1880 (A)
  misc. papers
  In Hofstra Univ. Library (Hempstead, N.Y.)

  misc. papers
  In Univ. of Rochester, Rush Rhees Library, Isaac Post Family
  Collection (Rochester, N.Y.)

CHILDREN'S TELEVISION WORKSHOP
  8 transcripts
  In Columbia Univ., Butler Library, Oral History Coll. (N.Y.)
  Transcripts of tape-recorded interviews with some of those
  principally responsible for the development of Children's
  Television Workshop and the creation of "Sesame Street."
  Participants recall 1966 discussions of how television might
  be made to serve preschool children, preliminary studies, the
  roles of the Carnegie Corporation, of Harold Howe II as U.S.
  Commissioner of Education, and of the Ford Foundation in
  advancing the concept and helping to finance it, the founding
  of the workshop and its staffing, and the emergence of the
  "Sesame Street" format, as well as the changing relationship
  of the workshop with National Educational Television, from
  which it became independent. Persons interviewed include
  David Connell, Joan Cooney, Robert Davidson, Barbara Finberg,
  Louis Hausman, Edward Meade, Lloyd Morrisett, and John White.

CIARDI, JOHN, 1916-   (poet)
  misc. papers, 1955-68. 260 items
  In Library of Congress, Manuscript Division (Washington, D.C.)
  Chiefly literary mss. in prose and verse, correspondence,
  notebooks, translations (The Divine Comedy), printed material
  and other papers. The prose mss. are principally drafts of

CIARDI, JOHN
   Ciardi's regular columns for SATURDAY REVIEW, and the poetry
   mss. include children's verse and other works in various
   stages of development.
   Additions to the collection are anticipated.

   misc. papers. 400 items
   In Library of Congress, Manuscript Division, Charles E.
   Feinberg Collection of John Ciardi (Washington, D.C.)
   Mss. and typescripts of poetry and prose, miscellaneous
   printed matter, and pictorial material. Approximately one-
   half of the collection is made up of the printer's copy of
   MID-CENTURY AMERICAN POETS (1950), edited by Ciardi, and
   correspondence and other writings associated with its
   production. Poets with correspondence relating to the
   volume include Elizabeth Bishop, Richard Eberhart, Randall
   Jarrell, Theodore Roethke, Muriel Rukeyser, Karl Shapiro,
   and Peter Viereck.

CLEMENS, SAMUEL LANGHORNE, 1835-1910   (A)
   misc. papers
   In Buffalo and Erie County Public Library (Buffalo, N.Y.)
   Includes original mss. of HUCKLEBERRY FINN (1884).

   misc. papers
   In DeGolyer Foundation Library (Dallas, Tex.)

   misc. papers and photographs
   In Detroit Public Library (Detroit, Mich.)

   misc. papers
   In Hartford Public Library (Hartford, Conn.)

   misc. papers
   In Harvard Univ., Houghton Library (Cambridge, Mass.)

   misc. papers, 1867-95. ca. 140 items
   In Henry E. Huntington Library (San Marino, Calif.)
   Letters (mainly to Mary J. Mason Fairbanks) and literary mss.

   misc. papers
   In Indiana Univ., Lilly Library (Bloomington, Ind.)

   misc. papers
   In Library of Congress (Washington, D.C.)

   misc. papers. ca. 2,000 items
   In Mark Twain Birthplace Memorial Shrine (Florida, Mo.)
   In part, transcripts and photocopies of papers. First
   editions of Clemens' books; related correspondence of

CLEMENS, SAMUEL LANGHORNE
   Clemens' family, associates; and other papers. Manuscript
by a professional copyist of THE ADVENTURES OF TOM SAWYER
(1876) with 15 holograph pages and many notes by Clemens,
and a few notes and corrections by William Dean Howells;
correspondence (8 items) of Clements and Moncure D. Conway
concerning the book; the contract with Chatto and Windus;
and statement of royalties (1877-87). Described in THE
TWAINIAN 9:1-2 (July-Aug. 1950). The manuscript of TOM
SAWYER is also described in Bernard DeVoto's MARK TWAIN AT
WORK (1942).

misc. papers
In Millicent Library (Fairhaven, Mass.)
Uncataloged collection of Clemens' letters and papers.

misc. papers
In Nook Farm Research Library (Hartford, Conn.)

misc. papers. ca. 75 items
In Princeton Univ. Library (Princeton, N.J.)
For description of this collection see PRINCETON UNIVERSITY
LIBRARY CHRONICLE 12:217-18.

misc. papers
In Public Library of Cincinnati and Hamilton County
(Cincinnati, Ohio)

misc. papers, 1872-1905. 61 items
In St. John's Seminary Library (Camarillo, Calif.)
Letters and other papers. Correspondents include Karl
Gerhardt, William Dean Howells, Otis Skinner, Charles W.
Stoddard, Emma Beach Thayer, and J. M. Tuohy.

misc. papers
In Univ. of California, Bancroft Library (Berkeley, Calif.)
Includes Clemens' correspondence, books and related material.

misc. papers
In Univ. of Rochester Library (Rochester, N.Y.)

misc. papers, 1872-1946. 2 ft.
In Univ. of Virginia Library (Charlottesville, Va.)
Correspondence, literary mss. and other papers of or relating
to Clemens. Includes mss. of THE JUMPING FROG (1903),
chapters from THE GILDED AGE (1874) and A TRAMP ABROAD (1880),
and other works; a biography (1885-86) of Clemens by his
daughter, Olivia Susan Clemens with his comments; and a diary
(1895-96) consisting of copies of family letters and notes
written while on tour to Australia, India, and South Africa.

CLEMENS, SAMUEL LANGHORNE
   Correspondents include James Tinkham Babb, Joseph L Blamire,
   George Hiram Brownell, S. Butler, Clara Spaulding Clemens,
   Cyril Clemens, J. B. Clemens, Jane Lampton Clemens, Olivia
   Langdon Clemens, Olivia Susan Clemens, Susan Langdon Crane,
   Dawson's Book Shop, Dodd, Mead and Co., Frederick A. Duneka,
   John Galsworthy, Frank Glenn, Edwin Grabhorn, Mr. Hall, Bret
   Harte, Mrs. Hatfield, Merle DeVore Johnson, Luther Samuel
   Livingston, Frank Mayo, Pamela Clemens Moffett, Capt. Mouland,
   Parke-Bernet Galleries, Inc., James Payn, David Anton Randall,
   George Routledge & Sons, Scribner Book Store, Ellen Kate
   Shaffer, Arthur Swann, Charles Dudley Warner, Carroll Atwood
   Wilson, Charles Erskine Scott Wood, and James McIntosh Wood.

   misc. papers
   In Univ. of Wisconsin Memorial Library, Brownell-Bassett
   Collection (Madison, Wisc.)

   misc. papers
   In Yale Univ., Beinecke Library (New Haven, Conn.)

   SAMUEL L. CLEMENS FAMILY COLLECTION, 1867-1909
   misc. papers. 584 items
   In Mark Twain Memorial (Hartford, Conn.)
   Correspondence, literary mss., documents, and other papers.
   Includes 17 mss. of Clemens, and a few by Lydia Sigourney,
   James Hammond Trumbull, and Charles Dudley Warner.
   Correspondents include Clara Langdon Clemens, Jane (Jean)
   Lampton Clemens, Olivia Langdon Clemens, Olivia Susan Clemens,
   Ida Langdon, and Isabel Lyons.

CLÉMENT, MARGUERITE (A)
   misc. papers. 28 items
   In Emporia State Univ. Library, May Massee Collection
   (Emporia, Kan.)
   Correspondence with May Massee.

COATSWORTH, ELIZABETH, 1893-   (A)*
   misc. papers and photographs
   In Bowdoin College Library (Brunswick, Me.)

COLMAN, HILA (A)
   papers, 1963-75. 6 ft.
   In Univ. of Oregon Library (Eugene, Or.)
   Papers include professional correspondence and mss. of books
   and articles.

COOPER, JAMES FENIMORE, 1789-1851 (A)
   misc. papers
   In American Antiquarian Society (Worcester, Mass.)

COOPER, JAMES FENIMORE
  misc. papers. 300 items
  In Lehigh Univ. Library (Bethlehem, Pa.)

  papers. 11 v. and 1 box
  In New York Historical Society (N.Y.)
  Correspondence and literary mss.

  misc. papers. 400 items
  In Univ. of Virginia Library (Charlottesville, Va.)

  misc. papers
  In Yale Univ., Beinecke Library (New Haven, Conn.)

CORMACK, MARIBELLE, 1902-   (A)
  papers, 1931-61. 10 ft.
  In Univ. of Oregon Library (Eugene, Or.)
  Mss. and correspondence for 18 books, chiefly juvenile, and
  original illustrations by Norman Price and Edward Shenton.

COSGRAVE, JOHN O'HARA, 1908-1968   (I)*
  papers, 1930-68. 12 ft.
  In Univ. of Oregon Library (Eugene, Or.)
  Papers include representation of practically all phases of
  Cosgrave's work: sketch books, book illustrations,
  advertising art, book jacket illustrations, Christmas cards
  and magazine illustrations. There is some professional
  correspondence, and a series of 43 letters, (1952-61), to
  Mary Silva Cosgrave. As Mary Silva, children's editor of
  Houghton Mifflin, Mrs. Cosgrave worked closely with Mary and
  Conrad Buff, May McNeer and Lynd Ward, Hans and Margaret Rey,
  and Julia Cunningham. Much of Miss Silva's correspondence
  is included with the collection.

COX, PALMER, 1840-1942   (I)*
  misc. papers, original art
  In Free Library of Philadelphia (Philadelphia, Pa.)

COX, WILLIAM ROBERT, 1901-   (A)
  papers, 1921-75. 15 ft.
  In Univ. of Oregon Library (Eugene, Or.)
  Papers include mss. of novels, stories for adolescents;
  screenplays, and television plays. Major correspondents are
  Lenniger Literary Agency, Paul Reynolds, Inc., Rogers Terrill
  Agency, Universal Publishing and Distributing Co., Bantam
  Books, Dodd, Mead and Co.

CRAIG, MARY FRANCIS, 1923-   (A)
  papers, 1958-77. 12 ft.
  In Univ. of Oregon Library (Eugene, Or.)

CRAIG, MARY FRANCIS
  Early work was written as Mary Francis Shura. Papers consist
  of mss. of 7 books and of stories and articles including her
  contributions to religious and confession magazines.
  Correspondence is with Atheneum Publishers, Alfred A. Knopf,
  Lenniger Literary Agency, and McIntosh and Otis, agents.

CRAIK, DINAH MULOCK, 1826-1887 (A)
  misc. papers
  In Univ. of California Libraries (Los Angeles, Calif.)

CRANE, WALTER, 1845-1915 (A,I)
  misc. papers. original art
  In Harvard Univ., Widener Library (Cambridge, Mass.)

  misc. papers. original art
  In Univ. of California Libraries (Los Angeles, Calif.)

  misc. papers. original art
  In Yale Univ., Beinecke Library (New Haven, Conn.)
  Collection contains books written and illustrated by Crane.

CREDLE, ELLIS, 1902-   (A,I)
  misc. papers, 1964-71. 1 ft.
  In Univ. of Oregon Library (Eugene, Or.)
  Correspondence, mostly with Thomas Nelson and Sons; literary
  mss., sketches, dummies, and related material for 5 books.

CROWELL, PERS, 1910-   (A,I)*
  papers, 1946-73. 4 ft.
  In Univ. of Oregon Library (Eugene, Or.)
  Correspondence with publishers, general correspondence
  relating to 7 of Crowell's books, drafts, and sketches.

CRUIKSHANK, GEORGE, 1792-1878 (I)*
  misc. papers. original art
  In Boston Univ. Library (Boston, Mass.)

  misc. papers. original art
  In Harvard Univ., Widener Library (Cambridge, Mass.)

  misc. papers
  In New York Public Library, Arents Collection (N.Y.)

  misc. papers. original art. ca. 1,500 items
  In Princeton Univ. Library (Princeton, N.J.)
  Correspondence, drawings, sketches and other items by or
  relating to the English artist.

  misc. papers. original art
  In Rosenbach Foundation Museum and Library (Philadelphia, Pa.)

CRUIKSHANK, GEORGE
  misc. papers and original art, 1824-72. 86 items
  In Univ. of Virginia Library (Charlottesville, Va.)
  Correspondence with authors, publishers and friends; pen,
  pencil and color sketches. The correspondence often includes
  sketches and relates to Cruikshank's works. Correspondents
  include George Mills, Charles Tilt, and John Wright.

  misc. papers. original art
  In Yale Univ., Beinecke Library, (New Haven, Conn.)

CULLEN, COUNTEE, 1903-1946 (A)
  misc. papers
  In Amistad Research Center (New Orleans, La.)

  papers. ca. 1,300 items
  In Atlanta Univ., Trevor Arnett Library (Atlanta, Ga.)
  Correspondence, literary mss., poems, articles, notes,
  postcards, proofs, and other papers, chiefly collected by
  Harold Jackman. Correspondents include Samuel Howard Archer,
  James Baldwin, Richmond Barthe, Arna Bontemps, Gwendolyn
  Brooks, Owen Dodson, Angelina Grimke, William Christopher
  Handy, Langston Hughes, Georgia Douglas Johnson, Claude McKay,
  Eslanda Goode Robeson, Paul Robeson, Charles Sebree, Era Bell
  Thompson, Leigh Whipper, and Clarence Cameron White.
  Described in an ANNOTATED BIBLIOGRAPHY OF THE DATED
  MANUSCRIPTS IN THE COUNTEE CULLEN COLLECTION IN THE TREVOR
  ARNETT LIBRARY by Lola B. Evans, Atlanta Univ. thesis (1959).

CUNNINGHAM, JULIA WOOLFOLK, 1916-   (A)*
  papers, 1957-72. 4 ft.
  In Univ. of Oregon Library (Eugene, Or.)
  Collection includes mss. of books and poems in various stages
  and personal and professional correspondence. Major
  correspondents are Collins-Knowlton-Wing, Inc., Mary Silva
  Cosgrave, Madeline L. Franklin, Houghton Mifflin, Margaret
  McElderry , Harcourt, Brace & World , Evaline Ness, and
  Pantheon Books, Inc.

DALY, MAUREEN
  see MCGIVERN, MAUREEN

DANIELS, GUY, 1919-   (A)
  papers, 1952-68. 1 ft.
  In Boston Univ. Library (Boston, Mass.)
  Correspondence, notes, typescripts of published and
  unpublished writings in variant drafts with holograph
  corrections and galleys, relating to Daniels' work translating
  children's literature from Russian, as literary critic and
  author.
  Additions to the collection are anticipated.

DAUGHERTY, CHARLES MICHAEL, 1914-   (A)
   mss. and correspondence. 1 ft.
   In Univ. of Oregon Library (Eugene, Or.)

DAUGHERTY, JAMES HENRY, 1889-1974 (A,I)*
   papers, 1930-74. 24 ft.
   In Univ. of Oregon Library (Eugene, Or.)
   Mss. of 10 books; 4 by Daugherty, 4 by Sonia Daugherty, and 2
   by Charles Daugherty; together with illustrations by
   James Daugherty for 30 books.

   original art. 111 items
   In Emporia State Univ. Library, May Massee Collection
   (Emporia, Kan.)
   Misc. artwork for: DANIEL BOONE (1926), ANDY AND THE LION
   (1938), DANIEL BOONE (1939), ABRAHAM LINCOLN (1943), THE
   PICNIC (1958).

D'AULAIRE, EDGAR PARIN
   see AULAIRE, EDGAR PARIN D'

DAVIS, RICHARD HARDING, 1864-1916 (A)
   papers, 1864-1916. 5 ft.   ca. 5,000 items
   In Univ. of Virginia Library (Charlottesville, Va.)
   Correspondence; in part, transcripts (typewritten); pieces
   from the diary (1865-79) of Davis' mother, Rebecca Harding
   Davis; mss. of Davis' plays and dramatizations by others
   from Davis' stories; agreements between Davis and various
   publishers; copyrights; notebooks, address books, accounts,
   notes, photos.

DAWSON, CARLEY (ROBINSON) (A)
   misc. papers, 1921-68. ca. 2 ft.
   In Univ. of Oregon Library (Eugene, Or.)
   Correspondence reflecting the involvement of Mrs. Dawson and
   her family with musicians, artists, writers, and society, and
   the cosmetics firm Mary Chess, Ltd. Persons mentioned include
   Brian Guinness, Juan Ramón Jiménez, Jack Love, Robert Lowell,
   and Alexis St. Leger. Correspondents incude Allan Dawson,
   Richard Hope Hawkins, Lura Chess Howard, Avery Robinson,
   Grace (Chess) Robinson, and other members of the Chess, Dawson
   and Robinson families.

DE ANGELI, MARGUERITE (LOFFT), 1889-   (A,I)*
   papers, 1935-75. 312 items
   In Free Library of Philadelphia (Philadelphia, Pa.)
   Misc. mss. and artwork for: TED AND NINA GO TO THE GROCERY
   STORE (1935), SKIPPACK SCHOOL (1938), THEE, HANNAH! (1940),
   ELIN'S AMERIKA (1941), TURKEY FOR CHRISTMAS (1944), BRIGHT
   APRIL (1946), JARED'S ISLAND (1947), BLACK FOX OF LORNE (1956),

DE ANGELI, MARGUERITE (LOFFT)
THE OLD TESTAMENT (1960), THE GOOSE GIRL (1964), FIDDLESTRINGS
(1974) and THE LION IN THE BOX (1975).
Additions to the collection are anticipated.

DEFOE, DANIEL, 1660?-1731   (A)
collection of letters, memorabilia and misc. papers
In Indiana Univ., Lilly Library (Bloomington, Ind.)

papers
In Johns Hopkins Univ. Library, Osler Collection (Baltimore,
Md.)

DE JONG, MEINDERT, 1910-   (A)*
misc. papers, 1933-56. 65 items
In Central Michigan Univ., Charles V. Park Library
(Mount Pleasant, Mich.)
Business correspondence received by De Jong from his
publishers and from his agent E. Nowell; 1 letter by De Jong;
mss. and drafts of his books, including THE BIG GOOSE AND THE
LITTLE DUCK (1938), DIRK'S DOG BELLO (1939), BELLS OF THE
HARBOR (1941), WHEELS OVER THE BRIDGE (1941), THE CAT THAT
WALKED A WEEK (1943), LITTLE STRAY DOG (1943), BILLY AND THE
UNHAPPY BULL (1946), GOOD LUCK DUCK (1950), THE TOWER BY THE
SEA (1950), SHADRACH (1953), THE HOUSE OF SIXTY FATHERS
(1956), THE MIGHTY ONES (1959); and reports (1938) of the
Federal Music Project.

DE LA MARE, WALTER JOHN , 1873-1956   (A)*
misc. papers, 1920-56. 155 items
In Syracuse Univ. Library (Syracuse, N.Y.)
Correspondence and 10 literary mss.

papers, 1918-56. 166 items
In Temple Univ. Library (Philadelphia, Pa.)
Correspondence, together with mss. of the poems "Defeat,"
"Drugged," "Reflections," and "On the Esplanade." Letters to
British authors St. John Adcock, Edward Meyerstein, and Thomas
Quayle; also Otto Kyllmann of Constable and Co., Ltd. Among
letters to Kyllmannn are a set of 14 concerned with
publication of POEMS FOR CHILDREN (1930). Includes carbon
copies of 12 letters from Kyllmann to De La Mare on the
same subject.

DENNIS, MORGAN   (A,I)
original art. 122 items
In Emporia State Univ. Library, May Massee Collection
(Emporia, Kan.)
Misc. artwork for: THE PUP HIMSELF (1943), THE DOG NEXT DOOR
(1950), SKIT AND SKAT (1951), LOST DOG JERRY (1952), HIMSELF

DENNIS, MORGAN
AND BURLAP ON TV (1954), THE DOG THAT COULD SWIM UNDER WATER
(1956).

DE REGNIERS, BEATRICE SCHENK (FREEDMAN), 1914-   (A)
misc. papers, 1963-68. 24 items
In Free Library of Philadelphia (Philadelphia, Pa.)
Misc. artwork and related materials for: THE LITTLE GIRL AND
HER MOTHER (1963), MAY I BRING A FRIEND? (1964), ABRAHAM
LINCOLN JOKE BOOK (1965), WILLY O'DWYER JUMPED IN THE FIRE
(1968).

DESMOND, ALICE CURTIS, 1897-   (A)
papers, 1931-71. 6 ft.
In Univ. of Oregon Library (Eugene, Or.)
Collection consists of mss. and related material for 21 books,
correspondence with publishers, and some original artwork.
Major correspondents include Dorothy Bryant of Dodd, Mead
and Co., and Doris Patee of Macmillan Co. Illustrations
include an original gouache of a koala by Sam Savitt.

DICKENS, CHARLES, 1817-1870 (A)
misc. papers, 1840-68. ca. 50 items
In Columbia Univ., Butler Library (N.Y.)
In part, transcripts. Letters, engravings, and caricatures
relating to Dickens. Includes an autograph letter from him
and copies of several Dickens' letters to the publishers
Lea and Blanchard.

misc. papers, 1835-70. 3 ft. ca. 800 items
In Free Library of Philadelphia (Philadelphia, Pa.)
Mainly letters written by author and collected from a variety
of sources by David Jacques Benoliel, William M. Elkins, and
others. Includes original mss. of 3 complete and 2
fragmentary dramatic sketches. Correspondents include
Countess of Blessington, Frederick Dickens, William Charles
Kent, John Leech, Mark Lemon, Daniel Maclise, Arthur Ryland,
Frank Stone, and Benjamin Webster.

misc. papers
In Harvard Univ., Houghton Library (Cambridge, Mass.)

misc. papers, 1832-70 ca. 1,250 items
In Henry E. Huntington Library (San Marino, Calif.)
Correspondence and original illustrations for OLD CURIOSITY
SHOP (1848), BARNABY RUDGE (1849), and other works. Includes
130 letters to Georgina Hogarth, 15 to Charles Kent, 92 to
Thomas Mitton, 81 to Frederick Ouvry, 55 to Richard Watson,
and 427 to W. H. Wills.

26

DICKENS, CHARLES
  misc. papers
  In Pierpont Morgan Library (N.Y.)

  misc. papers
  In Univ. of California Libraries (Los Angeles, Calif.)

  misc. papers
  In Univ. of California, William Andrews Clark Memorial
  Library (Los Angeles, Calif.)

  misc. papers, 1840-80. ca. 150 items
  In Univ. of Texas at Austin, Humanities Research Center
  Library (Austin, Tex.)
  Correspondence, literary mss., and illustrations. Includes
  the manuscript of THE IVY GREEN (1884); original
  illustrations for PICKWICK (1868) by Hablot Knight Browne and
  for various works by Joseph Clayton Clarke ("Kyd"), Charles
  Green, and Walter Crane; and letters referring to Dickens
  by Elizabeth Barrett Browning, Robert Browning, Thomas Carlyle,
  George Cruikshank, John Forster, and Kate Perugini.
  Correspondents include Gilbert A. Beckett, Henry Austin,
  Frederick Barnard, Marguerite Power, the Countess of
  Blessington, Robert Buchanan, George Cattermole, Chapmen &
  Hall, George Cruikshank, Lord Denman, Mrs. Catherine Gore,
  Richard Henry Horne, Walter Savage Landor, G. H. Lewes,
  Daniel Maclise, Frederick Marryat, Thomas Mitton, John Overs,
  Lord John Russell, George Augustus Sala, Marcus Stone, Joseph
  Story, Agnes Strickland, and Augustus Frederick Tracey.
  Described in a CATALOGUE OF THE VANDERPOEL DICKENS
  COLLECTION AT THE UNIVERSITY OF TEXAS, compiled by Sister
  Lucille Carr, 2nd ed. (1968).

  misc. papers
  In Yale Univ., Beinecke Library (New Haven, Conn.)

DODGE, MARY MAPES, 1831-1905 (A)
  misc. papers, 1866-91. 65 items
  In Henry E. Huntington Library (San Marino, Calif.)
  Letters to Horace Scudder.

DODGSON, CHARLES LUTWIDGE, 1832-1898 (A)
  misc. papers
  In Columbia Univ., Butler Library (N.Y.)

  misc. papers
  In Harvard Univ., Houghton Library (Cambridge, Mass.)
  For a description of this collection see THE HARCOURT AMORY
  COLLECTION OF LEWIS CARROLL IN THE HARVARD COLLEGE LIBRARY,
  Flora V. Livingston. Cambridge, Mass: Harvard Univ., 1932.

DODGSON, CHARLES LUTWIDGE
  misc. papers, 1848-97. 88 items
  In Henry E. Huntington Library (San Marino, Calif.)
  Letters to E. Gertrude Thomson and others.

  misc. papers and photographs
  In Rosenbach Foundation Museum and Library (Philadelphia, Pa.)

  misc. papers
  In Univ. of California Libraries (Los Angeles, Calif.)

DOYLE, RICHARD, 1824-1883 (I)
  original art
  In Duke Univ. Library (Durham, N.C.)
  Manuscript and water color illustration for THE MARVELLOUS
  HISTORY OF JACK THE GIANT KILLER (1842).

DU BOIS, WILLIAM PENE, 1916-   (A,I)
  original art. 23 items
  In Emporia State Univ. Library, May Massee Collection
  (Emporia, Kan.)
  Misc. artwork for: S.O.S. GENEVA (1939), THE FLYING LOCOMOTIVE
  (1941), JEXIUM ISLAND (1957)

DUFF, ANNIS (A)
  misc. correspondence. 25 items
  In Emporia State Univ. Library, May Massee Collection
  (Emporia, Kan.)

DUVOISIN, ROGER ANTOINE, 1904-   (A,I)*
DUVOISIN, LOUISE FATIO (A)*
  misc. papers, 1934-67. 1 box
  In Univ. of Oregon Library (Eugene, Or.)
  Literary mss. (20 items) including drafts, revisions,
  printer's copies, galley proofs, and sketches.

EBERLE, IRMENGARDE, 1898-   (A)*
  misc. papers, 1957-68. ca. 2 ft.
  In Univ. of Oregon Library (Eugene, Or.)
  Mss. and related material for 3 books; together with a
  collection of foreign editions of various titles.

EDGEWORTH, MARIA, 1767-1849 (A)
  misc. papers
  In Univ. of California Libraries (Los Angeles, Calif.)
  Literary mss. and correspondence.

  misc. papers
  In Yale Univ., Beinecke Library (New Haven, Conn.)

EGGLESTON, EDWARD, 1837-1902 (A)
  papers, 1804-1939. 12 ft.
  In Cornell Univ. Library, Collection of Regional History and
  University Archives (Ithaca, N.Y.)
  Correspondence, mss. of books and articles, notes for books,
  accounts, outlines and notes for sermons and newspaper
  clippings of book reviews and obituaries. Includes
  correspondence with publishers concerning royalties,
  copyrights and related matters; letters concerning historical
  and genealogical research; along with 48 letters to Robert
  Underwood Johnson, secretary of American Copyright League,
  concerning Eggleston's lobbying activities on behalf of
  international copyright law (1888-93).

EHRLICH, BETTINA, 1903- (A,I)*
  misc. papers. original art
  In Univ. of Oregon Library (Eugene, Or.)
  Manuscript and original illustrations for FOR THE LEG OF A
  CHICKEN (1960). Mss. consist of an original and a revised
  holograph text. There are 75 illustrations, 24 in water
  color.

EMERY, ANNE, 1907- (A)
  papers, 1941-77. 8 ft.
  In Univ. of Oregon Library (Eugene, Or.)
  Includes book mss., research materials, copies of published
  stories, and correspondence with publishers.

ETS, MARIE HALL, 1893- (A,I)*
  original art, 5 items
  In Emporia State Univ. Library, May Massee Collection
  (Emporia, Kan.)
  Misc. artwork for: IN THE FOREST (1944), MR. T. W. ANTHONY
  WOO (1951), NINE DAYS TO CHRISTMAS (1959), JUST ME (1965).

EVANS, EDMUND, 1826-1905 (wood engraver)
  misc. papers, ca. 1855-1910. ca. 150 items
  In Univ. of California Libraries (Los Angeles, Calif.)
  Correspondence addressed to Evans and to his son, Edmund
  Wilfred Evans, who carried on his father's work after 1905.
  The letters primarily concern business matters relating to
  color-printing, engraving, book illustration, and various
  English illustrators, but many contain personal and social
  messages to Evans and his family. Correspondents include
  H. K. Browne, Walter Crane, Birket Foster, Kate Greenaway,
  Joseph Pennell, John Tenniel, and other authors, illustrators,
  engravers and printers.

EVARTS, HAL GEORGE, 1915- (A)
  papers, 1936-76. 4 ft.

EVARTS, HAL GEORGE
  In Univ. of Oregon Library (Eugene, Or.)
  Includes professional correspondence, mss., and a travel
  diary (1936-37).

EYVIND, EARLE (I)
  original art. 108 items
  In Emporia State Univ. Library, May Massee Collection
  (Emporia, Kan.)
  Misc. artwork for: IN NORWAY (1948).

FALLS, CHARLES B. (I)
  misc. papers. original art. 82 items
  In Emporia State Univ. Library, May Massee Collection
  (Emporia, Kan.)
  Misc. artwork for: THE ABC BOOK (1923), THE FIRST 3000 YEARS
  (1960).

FARLEY, WALTER, 1915- (A)
  papers, 1941-66. ca. 2,500 items
  In Columbia Univ., Bulter Library (N.Y.)
  Editorial correspondence, notes, drafts, outlines,
  typescripts, and reviews of 21 novels in Farley's BLACK
  STALLION series, including THE BLACK STALLION (1941), THE
  GREAT DANE THOR (1966).

FERRIS, HELEN JOSEPHINE, 1890-1961 (editor)
  misc. papers. ca. 80 items
  In Franklin D. Roosevelt Library (Hyde Park, N.Y.)
  Letters from Eleanor Roosevelt and Maureen Corr to Miss Ferris
  and Miss Doumenjou, and articles relating to Mrs. Roosevelt
  and the Junior Literary Guild.

FIELD, EUGENE, 1850-1895 (poet)
  misc. papers. 800 items
  In Denver Public Library, Morris Collection (Denver, Colo.)
  145 letters from Field to others; approximately 250 letters
  to Field.

  misc. papers, 1872-94. 77 items
  In Henry E. Huntington Library (San Marino, Calif.)
  Correspondence and literary mss.

  misc. papers, 1873-95. 73 items
  In Jones Library (Amherst, Mass.)
  Letters to family members, friends, and business associates,
  and mss. of poems.

  misc. papers, 1855-1940. ca. 250 items
  In Missouri Historical Society (St. Louis, Mo.)

FIELD, EUGENE
   Chiefly proof sheets with notations and titles written in by
   Field, including a few corrected proof sheets signed by him;
   correspondence, theater programs, newspaper clippings; and a
   portfolio and notes of Field, corresponding secretary of the
   Missouri Press Association, 1898, giving a history of
   Missouri newspapers. Correspondents include Wilson Barrett,
   Samuel L. Clemens, Zee James (Mrs. Jesse James), Sol Smith
   Russell, and Francis Wilson.

   misc. papers, photographs
   In Newberry Library (Chicago, Ill.)

   misc. papers. 20 items
   In Southern Illinois Univ. Library (Edwardsville, Ill.)
   Poems, notes, and correspondence.

   misc. papers, 1872-1939. ca. 300 items
   In Univ. of Virginia Library, Clifton Waller Barrett Coll.
   (Charlottesville, Va.)
   Chiefly mss. of poems, together with family and professional
   correspondence. Page proofs of WITH TRUMPET AND DRUM (1892),
   Field's book, THE LOVE AFFAIRS OF A BIBLIOMANIAC (1896),
   and Douglas William Jerrold's play, "The Hamper of Wine," and
   photos. Correspondence relates to Field's family, book
   collecting, journalism, publication of his book, ECHOES FROM
   THE SABINE FARM (priv. printed 1891, published 1892), his
   poor health, and the death of his son, Melvin Gray Field.
   Correspondents include his wife, Julia Sutherland (Comstock)
   Field, their children, and Roswell Martin Field, Joseph
   Jefferson, Slason Thompson, and Francis Wilson.

   misc. papers, 1868-95. ca. 100 items
   In Washington Univ. Library (St. Louis, Mo.)
   Correspondence, notebook containing several early verses, mss.
   of 31 poems (many unpublished) and a manuscript catalog of
   Field's 5,000 volume library. Correspondents include James
   Field, Julia Field, Melvin Gray Field, Marcus Lemon Gray,
   Mark A. Hanna, Lynch Hanover, Beatrix Hawthorne, Julian
   Hawthorne, Thomas Hutchinson, Marie Jansen, Victor Fremont
   Lawson, Edmund Clarence Stedman, and George H. Yenowine.

FISHER, LEONARD EVERETT, 1924-   (A,I)*
   papers, 1936-68. 18 ft.
   In Univ. of Oregon Library (Eugene, Or.)
   Papers consist of: illustrations, including original drawings
   and paintings, overlays, dummies, and proofs; roughs and
   specifications for illustrations, including correspondence
   with publishers; mss. of books by Fisher, including drafts and
   final versions; correspondence with publishers, especially

FISHER, LEONARD EVERETT
Coward-McCann, Thomas Y. Crowell, Dial Press, Dodd, Mead and
Co., E. P. Dutton, Farrar, Straus and Giroux, Harper & Bros.,
Holiday House, Holt, Rinehart and Winston, Horn Book, Alfred
A. Knopf, Little, Brown and Co., Macmillan, William Morrow,
G. P. Putnam's Sons, Rand McNally, Random House, Science
Research Associates, Franklin Watts; correspondence with art
galleries and libraries, Leona J. Daniels, Richard B. Morris,
Sidney Offit, E. Brooks Smith and Fisher's family; exhibition
catalogues and broadcast tapes.

FITCH, FLORENCE MARY, 1875-1959 (A)
papers. 7 ft.
In Oberlin College Archives (Oberlin, Ohio)
Family correspondence, correspondence and clippings about Miss
Fitch's books for children, diaries, notes, talks, and
writings; correspondence from her years as a student at
Oberlin and in Munich and Berlin and her early teaching years
at Oberlin. Includes some letters written by a member of
Company C, 1st Regt., Ohio Light Artillery (1861-63).

FLACK, MARJORIE, 1897-1958 (A,I).
misc. papers, 1930-57. 3 ft.
In Univ. of Oregon Library (Eugene, Or.)
Original art, some correspondence and mss. dealing with 13
of her books. Also includes cartoons and art by Carl
Larsson and William Rose Benet as well as sketches of Miss
Flack's studio by Harrison Cady.

FLOETHE, LOUISE LEE, 1913-   (A)*
misc. papers. 1 ft.
In Univ. of Oregon Library (Eugene, Or.)
Collection consists of original mss., dummy, original art, and
minor correspondence concerning THE STORY OF LUMBER (1962).

FOLLETT, BARBARA NEWHALL, 1914- (A)
papers, 1919-39. ca. 2,000 items
In Columbia Univ., Butler Library (N.Y.)
Correspondence, literary mss. and memorabilia. Includes mss.
of THE HOUSE WITHOUT WINDOWS (1927), THE VOYAGE OF THE NORMAN
D (1928), LOST ISLAND (unpubl.), TRAVELS WITHOUT A DONKEY
(unpubl.), and numerous poems and stories; and letters from
Walter de la Mare.

FORBES, ESTHER, 1891-1968. (A)
misc. papers, 1945-67. 2 ft.
In American Antiquarian Society (Worcester, Mass.)
Notes for a history of witchcraft.

misc. papers, 1906-67. ca. 250 items
In Clark Univ. Library (Worcester, Mass.)

FORBES, ESTHER
  Manuscript of an unpublished novel entitled THE SONS OF UGO;
  some hundreds of pages of notes concerning the early history
  of Mass., carbon copy of typescript of the novel, PARADISE
  (1937); set of uncorrected printer's proofs of the novel,
  THE RUNNING OF THE TIDE (1948); and several hundred
  compositions, themes, essays, and stories, written by Miss
  Forbes from childhood through high school and college.

FOSTER, GENEVIEVE STUMP, 1893-   (A,I)*
  misc. papers. original art
  In Univ. of Oregon Library (Eugene, Or.)
  Collection includes 800 finished drawings for 12 published
  books and preliminary sketches and overlays for color
  illustrations. There is also some correspondence, plus
  printed reviews, photographs and memorabilia.

FOX, GARDNER FRANCIS, 1911- (A)
  papers, 1936-66. 8 ft.
  In Univ. of Oregon Library (Eugene, Or.)
  Prolific writer of detective comics, creator of the character
  Steve Malone, the first "Flash" comic and wrote text for issues
  of "Detective Batman," "Dr. Fate," "Spectre," and "Starman."
  He later created Ghost Rider for Magazine Enterprises. He
  writes under various pseudonyms, including Jefferson Cooper,
  Rod Gray, Kevin Matthews, Bart Somers, John Henry Morgan,
  James Kendriks, John Steele, Simon Majors, and Troy Conway.
  Under these and other names he writes sex novels, science
  fiction, and gothic romances. The papers consist of: mss. of
  books and short stories, and correspondence to and from the
  Lenniger Literary Agency; a collection of fan letters, and
  comic-book tear sheets. There is also a collection of comic
  books, western, mystery, adventure, and science fiction, pulp
  magazines, and comic-book fan periodicals.

FRANCHERE, RUTH MYERS (A)
  misc. papers, 1958-69. 1.5 ft.
  In Univ. of Oregon Library (Eugene, Or.)
  Papers consist of mss., galley proofs, research notes, and
  correspondence with Elizabeth M. Riley of Thomas Y. Crowell Co.

FREEMAN, DON, 1908- (A,I)*
  misc. papers. original art. 189 items
  In Emporia State Univ. Library, May Massee Collection
  (Emporia, Kan.)
  Misc. artwork for: CHUGGY AND THE BLUE CABOOSE (1951),
  FINDERS KEEPERS (1951), BILL BERGSON LIVES DANGEROUSLY (1954),
  MIKE'S HOUSE (1954), MOP TOP (1955), FLY HIGH, FLY LOW (1957),
  THE UNINVITED DONKEY (1957), THE NIGHT THE LIGHTS WENT OUT
  (1958), NORMAN THE DOORMAN (1959), COME AGAIN, PELICAN (1961),

FREEMAN, DON
  SKI PUP (1963).

FRIERMOOD, ELISABETH (HAMILTON), 1903-   (A)
  misc. papers, 1951-63. ca. 2 ft.
  In Univ. of Oregon Library (Eugene, Or.)
  Original mss. and related material for 9 books.

FRITZ, JEAN GUTTERY, 1915- (A)*
  misc. papers, 1962-69. 1 box
  In Univ. of Oregon Library (Eugene, Or.)
  Mss. in various stages.

GALLICO, PAUL, 1897-1976 (A)
  papers, 1922-69. ca. 10,000 items
  In Columbia Univ., Butler Library (N.Y.)
  Correspondence, literary papers, research notes, background
  materials, photos., documenting Gallico's literary career,
  beginning with sports columns written for THE DAILY NEWS in
  1922, and continuing through the publication of THE
  POSEIDON ADVENTURE (1969). Includes drafts, typescripts and
  proofs for all his major writings, among them, THE SNOW
  GOOSE (1941), THOMASINA (1957), MRS. 'ARRIS GOES TO PARIS
  (1958), THE HURRICANE STORY (1959), SCRUFFY (1962), and THE
  SILENT MIAOW (1964), in addition to hundreds of articles,
  essays, and stories which have appeared in COSMOPLITAN,
  ESQUIRE, THE SATURDAY EVENING POST, and other magazines.

GANNETT, RUTH, 1923- (I)*
  original art. 6 items
  In Emporia State Univ. Library, May Massee Collection
  (Emporia, Kan.)
  Misc. artwork for: MISS HICKORY (1946).

GARIS, HOWARD ROGER, 1873-1962 (A)
  misc. papers, 1910-62. 4 ft.
  In Syracuse Univ. Library (Syracuse, N.Y.)
  Correspondence, literary mss., memorabilia, and other papers,
  relating to Garis' "Uncle Wiggily" and other stories and to
  personal and family affairs.

GARST, DORIS SHANNON, 1899-   (A)
  papers, ca. 1937-73. ca. 5 ft.
  In Univ. of Wyoming Library, Division of Rare Books and
  Special Collections (Laramie, Wyo.)
  Correspondence, literary drafts, research notes, and speeches
  and lectures on writing.

GAY, ZHENYA (A,I)*
  original art. 345 items

GAY, ZHENYA
  In Emporia State Univ. Library, May Massee Collection
  (Emporia, Kan.)
  Misc. artwork for: THE INSECT WORLD (1947), LOOK! (1952),
  JINGLE JANGLE (1953), WONDERFUL THINGS! (1954), WHAT'S YOUR
  NAME? (1955), WHO IS IT? (1957), BITS AND PIECES (1958), THE
  METAMORPHOSES (1958), SMALL ONE (1958), THE NICEST TIME OF
  THE YEAR (1960), I'M TIRED OF LIONS (1961), WHO'S AFRAID?
  (1965).

GEISEL, THEODOR SEUSS, 1904- (A,I)*
  misc. papers, 1937-66
  In Univ. of California Library, Department of Special
  Collections (Los Angeles, Calif.)
  Approximately 35 titles with all of the related artwork,
  preliminary and final and with mss., notes, rough drafts. In
  addition, 1,000 pieces of ephemera, mostly clippings of
  political cartoons and advertisements by Geisel from the
  beginning of his career to the mid 1940's.

GIOVANNI, NIKKI, 1943-   (poet)
  papers, 1969-76. ca. 15 boxes
  In Boston Univ. Library, Department of Special Collections
  (Boston, Mass.)
  Printed material, photos., memorabilia, magazines, leaflets,
  pamphlets and broadsides containing poems and articles.
  Photo copies of writings by and about Nikki Giovanni, photos,
  posters and publicity material; business correspondence.

GOREY, EDWARD (ST. JOHN), 1925-   (I)
  original art
  In New Mexico State Univ. Library (Las Cruces, N.M.)

GRAMATKY, HARDIE, 1907-1979 (A,I)*
  misc. papers. 5 ft. 217 items
  In Univ. of Oregon Library (Eugene, Or.)
  Collection includes notebooks, sketch books, drawings, color
  illustrations, idea paintings, layouts, and mss. for: LOOPY
  (1941), NIKOS AND THE SEA GOD (1963) and LITTLE TOOT ON THE
  GRAND CANAL (1968).

GRAY, HAROLD, 1894-1968 (cartoonist)
  misc. original art. ca. 20 ft.
  In Boston Univ. Library, Special Collections (Boston, Mass.)
  Original pen and ink drawings of the strip "Little Orphan
  Annie" (1924-65).

GREENAWAY, KATE, 1846-1901 (I)*
  original art. 98 items
  In Detroit Public Library (Detroit, Mich.)

GREENAWAY, KATE
  Collection includes original drawings, watercolors, greeting
  and Christmas cards, bookplates, Minton tile, and wallpaper
  specimen.

  misc. papers. original art
  In Free Library of Philadelphia (Philadelphia, Pa.)
  Collection includes original watercolors and autograph letters

  misc. papers. original art
  In New York Public Library, Arents Collection (N.Y.)

  misc. papers. original art
  In Univ. of Southern Mississippi Library (Hattiesburg, Miss.)

GREY, ZANE, 1872-1939 (A)
  papers. 15 ft.
  In Ohio Historical Society (Columbus, Ohio)
  Mss., galley proofs, and comic strips of Grey's western novels
  and short stories, together with scrapbook of correspondence
  from readers and copies of Grey's articles on deep sea fishing.

GRINNELL, GEORGE BIRD, 1849-1938 (naturalist)
  misc. papers, 1876-1939. ca. 150 items
  In Nebraska State Historical Society (Lincoln, Neb.)
  Correspondence (1915-39), printed material (1876-1921) and
  other papers, relating to Indian history and culture, Indian
  fighters, the preparation and publication of historical books
  and articles, and location of historic sites.

GROVER, EULALIE OSGOOD, 1873-1958 (A)
  misc. papers. 12 items
  In Free Library of Philadelphia (Philadelphia, Pa.)
  Correspondence from Bertha C. Melcher and from Bertha L.
  Corbett to Mr. Grover.

HADER, ELMER STANLEY, 1889-1973 (A,I)*
HADER, BERTA HOERNER, 1890-1976 (A,I)*
  original art. 108 items
  In Emporia State Univ Library, May Massee Collection
  (Emporia, Kan.)
  Misc. artwork for: A MONKEY TALE (1929), LION CUB (1931),
  DOWN RYTON WATER (1941).

  papers, 1890-1976. 30 ft.
  In Univ. of Oregon Library (Eugene, Or.)
  Papers include mss., dummies, original illustrations and proofs
  of Elmer Stanley and Berta Hader.

HAENIGSEN, HARRY WILLIAM, 1900-   (A,I)
  original art, 1926-66
  In Univ. of Oregon Library (Eugene, Or.)
  Collection includes original artwork, proofs and clippings
  relating to "Our Bill," "Penny," PHOTOPLAY and MOTION PICTURE

HAGGARD, SIR HENRY RIDER, 1856-1925 (A)
  misc. papers, ca. 1866-1925. ca. 245 items
  In Columbia Univ., Butler Library (N.Y.)
  Letters to Haggard, Coulson Kernahan and many other prominent
  literary figures, relating to literary, publishing, social,
  and personal affairs. Correspondents include James M. Barrie,
  Hall Caine, Mrs. Patrick Campbell, J. Chamberlain, Wilkie
  Collins, Marie Corelli, Austin Dobson, Arthur Conan Doyle,
  Anthony Froude, John Galsworthy, Edmund Gosse, Anthony
  Hawkins, Andrew Lang, C. J. Longman, John E. Millais,
  William Morris, Ouida, Eden Phillpotes, Grant Richards,
  Rafael Sabatini, and John Tenniel.

  misc. papers, 1880-1925. ca. 215 items
  In Henry E. Huntington Library (San Marino, Calif.)
  Chiefly letters to Haggard by well-known writers, politicians,
  and publishers.

HALE, EDWARD EVERETT, 1822-1909 (A)
  papers. ca. 19 ft.
  In New York State Library (Albany, N.Y.)
  Correspondence, diaries (1834-1908), journals (1837-1909),
  sermons, lectures, notebooks, themes and other Harvard
  College papers, biographical material on Hale, scrapbooks
  and memorabilia.

(HALE, LUCRETIA PEABODY, 1820-1900) (A)
  Hale and Everett family papers, 1780-1967. 55 ft.
  In Smith College Library (Northampton, Mass.)
  Correspondence, diaries, speeches, lectures, biographical
  material, sermons, articles, stories, account books,
  scrapbooks, clippings, printed matter, photos, drawings,
  oil paintings, sketchbooks, writings, memorabilia, and
  other papers.
  Described in library's ANNUAL REPORT OF THE DIRECTOR, 1961-65.

HALL, ROSALYS HASKELL, 1914-   (A)
  misc. papers, 1954-68. 1 ft.
  In Univ. of Oregon Library (Eugene, Or.)
  Includes mss. and related material for 6 books, correspondence
  with editors, publishers and illustrators, copies of 8 books.
  Original illustrations and dummies for Hall books are in the
  Kurt Werth collection.

HANDFORTH, THOMAS SCHOFIELD, 1897-1948 (A,I)*
  papers, 1916-48. 5 ft.
  In Tacoma Public Library (Tacoma, Wash.)
  Letters from Handforth to his mother, Ruby Edwardine (Shera)
  Handforth, and sister-in-law, diaries, mss. of several
  books, prints, sketches, drawings, lithographs, and paintings.

HARPER, THEODORE ACLAND, 1871-1942 (A)
  misc. papers, 1928-35. 1.5 ft.
  In Univ. of Oregon Library (Eugene, Or.)
  Mss. of THE MUSHROOM BOY (1924) and SINGING FEATHERS (1925).

HARPER & ROW PUBLISHERS
  records, 1935-65. ca. 23,000 items
  In Columbia Univ., Butler Library (N.Y.)
  Editorial files documenting the publication of works.

HARPER BROS.
  papers. 34 boxes
  In Princeton Univ. Library (Princeton, N.J.)
  Correspondence and other business papers from the company's
  files. Writers for children represented include Countee
  Cullen, Booth Tarkington, etc.

HAWKES, CLARENCE, 1869-1954 (A)
  papers, 1890-1934
  In Forbes Library (Northampton, Mass.)
  32 mss. of books, 6 scrapbooks of biographical material;
  several hundred pieces of correspondence to Mr. Hawkes
  including letters from Thornton W. Burgess, Ernest T. Seton,
  Mary Mapes Dodge, Thomas W. Higginson, James Whitcomb Riley,
  Gene Stratton-Porter.

HAWTHORNE, NATHANIEL, 1804-1864 (A)
  misc. papers
  In Bowdoin College Library (Brunswick, Me.)
  Misc. letters to William B. Pike and Horatio Bridge.

  misc. papers
  In Concord Free Public Library (Concord, Mass.)

  misc. papers
  In Harvard Univ., Houghton Library (Cambridge, Mass.)

  misc. papers
  In Pierpont Morgan Library (N.Y.)

  misc. papers, 1837-1903. 86 items
  In St. Lawrence Univ. Library, Milburn Family Collection
  (Canton, N.Y.)

HAWTHORNE, NATHANIEL
    Correspondence, literary mss. and other papers. Includes mss.
    of LEAMINGTON SPA (n.d., ca. 1920), fragments from notebooks
    and bibliographical stories, 14 pages of a diary (1854-55)
    kept by Sophia Hawthorne in England.

    misc. family papers, 1659-1888. ca. 215 items
    In Univ. of Virginia Library (Charlottesville, Va.)
    Correspondence, literary mss. and other papers (chiefly
    after 1813). Material pertains to Hawthorne's days at the
    customhouse in Boston (1839-40), in the District of Salem and
    Beverly (1874-54), and as consul at Liverpool (1853-60).
    Includes family correspondence and letters to publishers; a
    few early papers of Hawthorne's ancestors; mss. of A WONDER
    BOOK FOR GIRLS AND BOYS (1852), and Hawthorne-Longfellow
    correspondence.

HAYWOOD, CAROLYN, 1898-   (A,I)*
    misc. papers, 1963-74. 194 items
    In Free Library of Philadelphia (Philadelphia, Pa.)
    Misc. artwork and related material for: A SUNDAE WITH JUDY
    (1949); mss. of HERE COMES THE BUS (1963), ROBERT ROWS THE
    RIVER (1965), EDDIE THE DOG HOLDER (1966), BETSY AND MR.
    KILPATRICK (1967), TAFFY AND MELISSA MOLASSES (1969), C. IS
    FOR CUPCAKE (1974).
    Additions to the collection are anticipated.

HENTOFF, NAT, 1925-   (A)
    papers, 1957-69. 7 ft.
    In Boston Univ. Library (Boston, Mass.)
    Research notes, variant drafts of Hentoff's works, with
    corrections, galleys and tapes, primarily of national figures
    speaking on current problemes. The latter include Joan Baez,
    James Farmer, Bayard Rustin, Roy Wilkins, and Whitney Young.

HIGGINSON, THOMAS WENTWORTH, 1823-1911 (A)
    misc. papers, 1844-1911. 40 items
    In American Academy of Arts and Letters Library (N.Y.)
    Correspondence chiefly relating to the National Institute of
    Arts and Letters and the American Academy of Arts and Letters,
    and mss. of Higginson's poems. Names prominently mentioned
    are Julia Ward Howe and Edith Wharton.

    misc. papers, 1868-1906. 55 items
    In Duke Univ. Library (Durham, N.C.)
    Letters by Higginson, mainly relating to literary and personal
    matters and to his lectures. Correspondents include William
    Bliss Carman, Daniel Coit Gilman, Julia Ward Howe, Charles
    Henry Miller, John Codman Ropes.

HIGGINSON, THOMAS WENTWORTH
  misc. papers
  In Harvard Univ., Houghton Library (Cambridge, Mass.)

  misc. papers, 1848-92. 133 items
  In Henry E. Huntington Library (San Marino, Calif.)
  Correspondence and literary mss. Includes two versions of
  THE LIFE OF JOHN GREENLEAF WHITTIER (1902) and THE LIFE OF
  BIRDS. Correspondents include Thomas Bailey Aldrich, Oliver
  Wendell Holmes, James Russell Lowell, Theodore Parker, and
  John Greenleaf Whittier.

  papers, 1855-60. 169 items
  In Kansas State Historical Society (Topeka, Kan.)
  Correspondence,telegrams, accounts, bills, receipts, and
  other papers relating chiefly to Free-State emigration to
  Kansas, aid to settlers, and border troubles, Described in
  the SIXTEENTH BIENNIAL REPORT OF THE KANSAS STATE HISTORICAL
  SOCIETY, 1907-08, p. 141-43.

HILL, DONNA M. (A,I)
  original art. 7 items
  In Emporia State Univ. Library, May Massee Collection
  (Emporia, Kan.)
  Misc. artwork for: NOT ONE MORE DAY (1957).

HOGNER, NILS, 1893-1970 (I)*
  papers, 1939-69. 8 ft.
  In Univ. of Oregon Library (Eugene, Or.)
  Papers consist of original illustrations, mss., dummies, and
  galley proofs for books by Dorothy Childs Hogner and others.

HOLBERG, RUTH LANGLAND, 1889-   (A)
  misc. papers, 1923-68. 4 ft.
  In Univ. of Oregon Library (Eugene, Or.)
  Papers consist of 23 book mss., some in several stages, mss. of
  magazine articles and stories, a private journal written in
  the 1920's and 1930's, and correspondence with editors and
  publishers,particularly Jean Poindexter Colby, Thomas Y.
  Crowell, Houghton Mifflin.

HOLBROOK, STEWART HALL, 1893-1964 (A)
  papers, 1904-64. 45 ft.
  In Univ. of Washington Library (Seattle, Wash.)
  In part, photocopies. Correspondence, diary, scrapbooks,
  notes, notebooks, research material, mss. of writings,
  speeches, reviews and other papers relating to Holbrook's
  career as journalist and free-lance writer in Seattle and
  Portland, his activities prior to World War II as an actor
  and baseball player, Pacific Coast journalism, and literary
  affairs.

HOLLING, HOLLING CLANCY, 1900–   (A,I)
  misc. papers, 1955-56. 1 box
  In Univ. of Oregon Library (Eugene, Or.)
  Correspondence, mss., galley proofs, publisher's dummy, and
  publicity relating to Holling's book, PAGOO (1957).

HONNESS, ELIZABETH HOFFMAN, 1904–   (A)
  misc. papers, 1957-66. 8 items
  In Free Library of Philadelphia (Philadelphia, Pa.)
  Misc. artwork and related material for: MYSTERY IN THE
  SQUARE TOWER (1957), MYSTERY OF THE SECRET MESSAGE (1961),
  MYSTERY OF THE PIRATE'S GHOST (1966).

HUGHES, LANGSTON, 1902-1967 (poet)
  misc. papers, 1928-67. 41 items
  In Boston Univ. Library, Department of Special Collections
  (Boston, Mass.)
  Letters written by Hughes to Leroi Jones, Clarence Major,
  Richard Nugent, Herbert Rock, Jules Schwerin, and Arthur
  Spingarn; mss. of poems and lyrics; printed items relating
  to Hughes.

  misc.papers
  In Fisk Univ. Library (Nashville, Tenn.)
  papers, 1926-67. 4 ft. ca. 4,500 items
  In New York Public Library, Schomburg Collection (N.Y.)
  Correspondence; mss., typescripts and drafts of books,
  articles, plays, poems, short stories, songs, and other
  writings; reviews of and by Hughes; articles, obituaries,
  sketches, and other biographical material; speeches,
  recordings, clippings, announcements, printed programs,
  leaflets, and other material relating to personal
  appearances, radio and television braodcasts and other
  programs, activities, and events in which Hughes participated
  or was the subject or in which his work was presented;
  information on sources of Hughes' material in other
  institutions; and miscellaneous material relating to Hughes.

  misc. papers
  In Univ. of Kansas, Kenneth Spencer Research Library
  (Lawrence, Kan.)

  misc. papers
  In Yale Univ., Beinecke Library (New Haven, Conn.)

HUNTER, KRISTIN (EGGLESTON), 1931–   (A)
  misc. papers. 2 items
  In Free Library of Philadelphia (Philadelphia, Pa.)
  Mss. of chapter 5 of THE SOUL BROTHERS AND SISTER LOU
  (1968); typescript of BOSS CAT (1971).

HUNTINGTON, HARRIET ELIZABETH, 1909-   (A)
  misc. papers, 1964-75. 3 ft.
  In Univ. of Oregon Library (Eugene, Or.)
  Collection includes mss. or dummies of several books with
  text and photographs by Miss Huntington.

HYDE, MARGARET OLDROYD, 1917-   (A)
  misc. papers, 1953. 21 items
  In Free Library of Philadelphia (Philadelphia, Pa.)
  Misc. artwork and related material for: FLIGHT TODAY AND
  TOMORROW (1953).

HYNDMAN, JANE ANDREWS (LEE), 1912-1978 (A)
  papers, 1947-78. 12 ft.
  In Univ. of Oregon Library (Eugene, Or.)
  Papers consist of mss. of books and articles, galley
  proofs, notes, and correspondence with editors and
  publishers. Major correspondents are Dodd, Mead (Dorothy
  M. Bryan), Doubleday (Margaret Lesser), Gladys Spicer
  Fraser, Junior Literary Guild (Helen Ferris), Alfred A.
  Knopf, Longmans, Green (Bertha Gunterman), Arnold Madison,
  Teri Martini, Julian Messner (Gertrude Blumenthal).
  Collection of the author's published works and three
  interview tapes; John McCaffery with Phyllis A. Whitney on
  WILLOW HILL (1947), and with Lee Wyndham on THE CANDY
  STRIPERS (1958) and on "By-products of Authorship",
  Christian Writers and Editors Conference, July, 1962 also
  included.

JACKSON, HELEN MARIA (FISKE) HUNT, 1831-1885 (A)
  misc. papers, 1852-57. 94 items
  In Henry E. Huntington Library (San Marino, Calif.)
  Mss. of literary works and letters to Charles Dickens, Mr.
  Jeffs, and others.

  misc. papers, 1837-84. 33 items
  In Jones Library (Amherst, Mass.)
  Letters to friends and business associates.

JANE, MARY CHILDS, 1909-   (A)
  papers, 1950-72. 2 ft.
  In Univ. of Maine Library (Orono, Me.)
  Mss. of writings and galley proofs.
  Additions to the collection are anticipated.

JARRELL, RANDALL, 1914-1965 (poet)
  misc. papers
  In New York Public Library, Research Division, Berg
  Collection (N.Y.)

JARRELL, RANDALL
  misc. papers
  In Univ. of North Carolina Library (Greensboro, N.C.)

JEWETT, SARAH ORNE, 1849-1909 (A)
  misc. papers, 1859-1904. 23 items
  In Boston Public Library (Boston, Mass.)
  Correspondence, poems, writing practice book, and address
  book.

  misc. papers, 1869-1908. 140 items
  In Colby College Library (Waterville, Me.)
  In part, transcripts (typewritten) and photocopies.
  Correspondence, literary mss., photos., printed matter. The
  largest groups of letters are those to Horace Scudder and
  William Dean Howells.
  Index to letters published in COLBY LIBRARY QUARTERLY
  (Sept, 1959).

  misc. papers, ca. 1870-79. 72 items
  In Columbia Univ., Butler Library (N.Y.)
  Letters written to Miss Jewett, chiefly personal, but with a
  few relating to the publication of her stories.
  Correspondents inlcude Ellen Emerson, William Dean Howells,
  Charles C. Hoyt, James R. Osgood, and Horace Scudder.

  misc. papers. 506 items
  In Harvard Univ., Houghton Library (Cambridge, Mass.)
  Mss. representing most of Miss Jewett's published literary
  works with a number of her unpublished stories and articles.
  For a description of this collection see HARVARD ALUMNI
  BULLETIN. 35:474-76 (1933).

  misc. papers
  In Syracuse Univ. Library (Syracuse, N.Y.)

JOHNSON, FERD, 1905-   (cartoonist)
  original art, 1943-1967. ca. 3,400 items
  In Boston Univ. Library (Boston, Mass.)
  Original pen and ink drawings, proofs and sketches for the
  syndicated comic strips "Moon Mullins," "Texas Slim," and
  "Buzzy."

JONES, ELIZABETH ORTON, 1910-   (A,I)*
  misc. papers. original art, 1925-78. 7 ft.
  In Univ. of Oregon Library (Eugene, Or.)
  Includes 38 prints (drypoint with aquatint), original
  illustrations for 11 books and miscellaneous artwork.

JONES, HAROLD, 1904-   (A,I)*
misc. papers, 1937-58. 1 ft.
In Univ. of Oregon Library (Eugene, Or.)
Correspondence, book dummies, original illustrations, and
other papers. Includes 29 letters from Walter de la Mare.

JOSEPH, NANINE, 1890-1976 (literary agent)
papers. 10.5 ft.
In Univ. of Oregon Library (Eugene, Or.)
Collection comprised of: correspondence with authors and
clients, including Lucy Herndon Crockett, Lorena A. Hickok,
Barbara and Myrick Ebben Land, Maud Hart and Delos Lovelace,
Adele Gutman Nathan, and Gray Johnson and Lynn Poole.

KEITH, ALICE, 1890-1962 (educator)
papers, 1906-62. 3 v., 3 boxes, 1 package
In State Historical Society of Wisconsin (Madison, Wisc.)
Pioneer in educational broadcasting, music teacher, and
founder and director of the National Academy of Broadcasting.
Correspondence, articles and addresses dealing with
education, scripts from CBS's "American School of the Air,"
and the National Academy of Broadcasting's "Music in the Air,"
press releases and printed material concerning educational
broadcasting of the NAOB, and memorabilia. Letters are
mostly personal, but the group from the 1930's shows Miss
Keith's efforts to become recognized as the first educational
broadcaster.

KENT, ROCKWELL, 1882-1971 (I)
papers, ca. 1904-65. 4,550 items
In Columbia Univ., Butler Library (N.Y.)
Miscellaneous correspondence, original mss., drawings,
sketches, architectural drawings, illustrations, watercolors,
lithographs, and proofs, Kent's own books and others
illustrated by him, and drawings for advertising, bookplates,
magazines, posters, and other works.

KETCHAM, HANK, 1920-   (cartoonist)
papers, 1951-65. ca. 3,000 items
In Boston Univ. Library (Boston, Mass.)
Original drawings of the cartoon strip, "Dennis the Menace,"
publicity materials, memorabilia, and other related papers.
Additions to the collection are anticipated.

KIPLING, RUDYARD, 1865-1936 (A)
misc. papers. 4 ft. ca. 600 items
In Cornell Univ. Library, Department of Rare Books (Ithaca,
N.Y.)
Correspondence (1866-1935) concerning Kipling's works,
sketches, clippings, poems, articles, literary mss. including

KIPLING, RUDYARD
an unpublished four-line verse in Kipling's hand, and photos;
together with letters and mss. of Edmonia Taylor Hill and
some members of Kipling's family.

misc. papers
In Harvard Univ., Widener Library (Cambridge, Mass.)

misc. papers. ca. 150 items
In Library of Congress, Rare Book Division (Washington, D.C.)
Forms part of the William Montelle Carpenter Kipling
Collection. Letters, stories, poems, sketches, corrected
galley proofs, cartoons, printer matter, photos, and
memorabilia. Literary mss. include the earlies draft of
"Mowgli's Brothers," THE ELEPHANT AND THE LARK'S NEST,
"William the Conqueror," A CELEBRITY AT HOME, "The Song of
the Women," THE NIGHT OF POWER, "L'Envoi," and TO THESE
PEOPLE. Corrected galley proofs include THE SHIP THAT FOUND
HERSELF, A TOUR OF INSPECTION, FROM SEA TO SEA (1899),
MRS. BATHURST, THE DAY'S WORK, THE CHILD OF CALAMITY,
"Among the Railway Folk," "The Elephant's Child," "The
Beginning of the Armadillos," and "The Sing-Song of Old Man
Kangaroo." Described in the ANNUAL REPORT OF THE LIBRARIAN
OF CONGRESS FOR THE FISCAL YEAR ENDING JUNE 30, 1941.

misc. papers, 1878-1932. 1 box
In Univ. of California, Bancroft Library (Berkeley, Calif.)
Correspondence, poem, and galley proof of the short story
"The King's Ankus" (1895); letters about Kipling written by
his mother, Alice (MacDonald) Kipling, Max Beerbohm, Lionel
C. Dunsterville, and Max Farrand; caricature of Kipling by
Beerbohm; and essay on Kipling by Andrew Lang.

misc. papers
In Univ. of California, General Library (Davis, Calif.)

misc. papers
In Univ. of California, William Andrews Clark Memorial Library
(Los Angeles, Calif.)

KNIGHT, RUTH ADAMS, 1894-1974 (A)
misc. papers, 1938-71. 10 ft.
In Univ. of Oregon Library (Eugene, Or.)
She created the radio series, "Brave Tomorrow," and wrote for
network programs, notably "Aunt Jenny's Real Life Stories."
Also wrote non-fiction books for women, stories for young
people, and television scripts. Collection of mss. reflects
all these aspects of her career. Correspondence is minor.

KNOPF (ALFRED A.) INC., NEW YORK
  records, 1930-61. 28 boxes
  In New York Public Library, Research Division (N.Y.)
  Mss. rejection correspondence (1939-43); mss. control
  records and readers' reports (1930-37); reviews clipping
  file; and mss. control records (ca. 1952-61) for Children's
  Books Dept.

KREDEL, FRITZ, 1900-   (I)*
  papers. original art
  In Yale Univ., Beinecke Library (New Haven, Conn.)

KUMIN, MAXINE WINOKUR, 1925-   (A)
  papers, 1960-68. ca. 3 ft.
  In Boston Univ. Library (Boston, Mass.)
  Correspondence, biographical material, notes and outlines,
  typescripts of Mrs. Kumin's writings with holograph
  corrections, galleys, clippings, and other papers,
  relating to her literary career.
  Additions to the collection are anticipated.

LAMPMAN, EVELYN (SIBLEY), 1907-   (A)
  papers, 1948-75. 6 ft.
  In Univ. of Oregon Library (Eugene, Or.)
  Correspondence with publishers, and book mss.

LANG, ANDREW, 1844-1912 (A)
  misc. papers
  In Indiana Univ., Lilly Library (Bloomington, Ind.)

LARCOM, LUCY, 1824-1893 (editor)
  misc. papers, 1859-90. 51 items
  In Henry E. Huntington Library (San Marino, Calif.)
  Literary mss. and letters to James T. Fields and others.

  misc. papers. ca. 1,200 items
  In Massachusetts Historical Society Library, Daniel Dulaney
  Addison Collection (Boston, Mass.)
  Correspondence, diary, and literary mss. of Miss Larcom,
  collected by Addison for use in writing LIFE AND LETTERS OF
  LUCY LARCOM (1894). The correspondence (1853-92) between
  Miss Larcom and John Greenleaf Whittier reveals his role as
  adviser, collaborator and personal friend, and deals with
  literary, editorial, and personal matters, criticism of her
  writing, and members of their literary circle. Includes
  publisher's accounts and communications relating to Miss
  Larcom's contributions and to her work as editor of OUR YOUNG
  FOLKS magazine. Other correspondents include Phillips
  Brooks, Annie and James T. Fields, and Esther Hamilton.

LATHAM, JEAN LEE, 1902-   (A)*
  misc. papers, ca. 1947-55. 1 box
  In West Virginia Univ. Library (Morgantown, W. Va.)
  Typescript copies of CARRY ON, MR. BOWDITCH (1955),
  TRAIL BLAZER OF THE SEAS (1956), THIS DEAR-BOUGHT LAND
  (1957).

LAWSON, ROBERT, 1892-1957 (A,I)*
  original art. 47 items
  In Emporia State Univ. Library, May Massee Collection
  (Emporia, Kan.)
  Misc. artwork for: FROM THE HORN OF THE MOON (1931),
  RABBIT HILL (1944), AT THAT TIME (1947).

  original art
  In Free Library of Philadelphia (Philadelphia, Pa.)
  Misc. artwork and related material for: THE WONDERFUL
  ADVENTURES OF LITTLE PRINCE TOOFAT (1922), THE WEE MEN OF
  BALLYWOODEN (1930), FROM THE HORN OF THE MOON (1931),
  THE ROVING LOBSTER (1931), PEIK (1932), THE UNICORN WITH
  SILVER SHOES (1932), THE HURDY-GURDY MAN (1933), HAVEN'S END
  (1933), THE TREASURE OF THE ISLE OF MIST (1934), THE GOLDEN
  HORSESHOE (1935), DRUMS OF MONMOUTH (1935), THE STORY OF
  FERDINAND (1936), UNDER THE TENT OF THE SKY (1937), FOUR &
  TWENTY BLACKBIRDS (1937), MIRANDA IS A PRINCESS (1937), MR.
  POPPER'S PENGUINS (1938), ONE FOOT IN FAIRYLAND (1938),
  PILGRIM'S PROGRESS (1939), BEN AND ME (1939), GAILY WE
  PARADE (1940), JUST FOR FUN (1940), THEY WERE STRONG AND
  GOOD (1940), I DISCOVER COLUMBUS (1941), AESOP'S FABLES
  (1941), THE STORY OF SIMPSON AND SAMPSON (1941), POO-POO AND
  THE DRAGONS (1942), ADAM OF THE ROAD (1942), PRINCE PRIGIO
  (1942), THE CROCK OF GOLD (1942), WATCHWORDS OF LIBERTY (1943),
  THE LITTLE WOMAN WANTED NOISE (1943), COUNTRY COLIC (1944),
  MR. WILMER (1945), GREYLOCK AND THE ROBINS (1946), AT THAT
  TIME (1947), MR. TWIGG'S MISTAKE (1947), ROBBUT: A TALE OF
  TAILS (1948), DICK WHITTINGTON & HIS CAT (1949), THE
  FABULOUS FLIGHT (1949), SMELLER MARTIN (1950), MCWHINNEY'S
  JAUNT (1951), EDWARD, HOPPY AND JOE (1952), MR. REVERE AND
  I (1953), THE TOUGH WINTER (1954), CAPTAIN KIDD'S CAT (1956),
  THE GREAT WHEEL (1957).

LEAR, EDWARD, 1812-1888 (I)
  misc. papers. original art
  In Harvard Univ., Houghton Library (Cambridge, Mass.)

  misc. papers. original art
  In Yale Univ., Beinecke Library (New Haven, Conn.)

LEE, MANNING DE VILLENEUVE, 1894-   (A,I)*
  original art. 17 items

LEE, MANNING DE VILLENEUVE
In Emporia State Univ. Library, May Massee Collection
(Emporia, Kan.)
Misc. artwork for: THE BLACK ARROWHEAD (1929), THE
DISAPPEARANCE OF ANNE SHAW (1930), FELITA (1932), GRAY
CAPS (1932), THE STARS OF SABRA (1932).

papers of Manning and Tina Lee, 1926-1961. 7 ft.
In Univ. of Oregon Library (Eugene, Or.)
Includes original illustrations, book mss. and correspondence

LEFFINGWELL, ROBERT (cartoonist)
papers. original art, 1892-1972. ca. 3,400 items
In Boston Univ. Library (Boston, Mass.)
Original pen and ink drawings, hand colored proofs and trial
sketches for the comic strips "Little Joe" and "Ze
Gen'ral;" correspondence; financial records; manuscript of
one poem.

LEIGHTON, MARGARET CARVER, 1896-   (A)*
papers, 1937-1960. 6 ft., including 1,000 letters
In Univ. of Oregon Library (Eugene, Or.)
Papers consist of mss., galley proofs, and correspondence
relating to 15 of her books. A major series of
correspondence is with Wilma K. McFarland, editor of THE
PORTAL and CHILD LIFE, 1937-47.

L'ENGLE, MADELEINE, 1918-   (A)*
papers, ca. 1930-   3 ft.
In Wheaton College Library (Wheaton, Ill.)
Mss. both holograph and typewritten, published and
unpublished with alterations of the following: CIRCLE OF
QUIET (1972), SUMMER OF THE GREAT-GRANDMOTHER (1974), DRAGONS
IN THE WATER (1976), IRRATIONAL SEASON (1977), SEVERED WASP
(unfinished). Transcripts of commencement and other
addresses; correspondence and letters (1976-   );
composition books (ca. 1930-   ); children's artwork and
letters responding to her books; photographs and artwork done
by Miss L'Engle.
Additions to the collection are anticipated.

LENNIGER LITERARY AGENCY
papers, 1926-75. 45 ft., including about 36,000 letters
In Univ. of Oregon Library (Eugene, Or.)
Founded by August Lenniger in 1923. Papers include
company ledgers and correspondence of August Lenniger, Edith
Margolis with agency clients and publishers. Letters concern
editing and sales of mss., requirements and house rules of
publishers, the state of the literary market, and personal
problems of writers. Writers include Irving and Ruth Adler,

LENNIGER LITERARY AGENCY
  Jules Archer, Peggy O'More Blocklinger, Helen Bratton,
  Anne Emery, Pearl Gishler, Edward A. Herron, Walt Morey,
  Denise Royal, Eva Rutland, William Irvin Severn, and Emma
  Gelders Sterne.

LENSKI, LOIS, 1893-1974 (A,I)*
  misc. papers, ca. 1900-74. 515 items
  In Amos Memorial Library (Sidney, Ohio)
  Correspondence, literary mss., galley proofs with corrections
  of WE LIVE IN THE NORTH (1965), original lithographs,
  linoleum prints, woodcuts, and other illustrations, taped
  interviews, recordings, photos, printed matter, autographed
  books, and miscellaneous material.

  misc. papers, 1900-70. 5 ft.
  In Capital Univ. Library (Columbus, Ohio)
  In part, transcripts and photocopies. Correspondence,
  diaries, biographical material, working notes and outlines,
  speeches, lectures, interviews, songs, poems, radio scripts,
  tape recordings, sketches and other artwork, published
  works, awards, mementos, clippings, and photos.

  misc. papers. photographs. original art
  In Emporia State Univ, William Allen White Library
  (Emporia, Kan.)

  misc. papers. original art
  In Florida State Univ. Library (Tallahassee, Fla.)
  For a detailed description of the collection see THE LOIS
  LENSKI COLLECTION IN THE FLORIDA STATE UNIVERSITY (1966).

  misc. papers, 1935-70. ca. 4 ft. ca. 470 items
  In Illinois State Univ. Library (Normal, Ill.)
  In part, photocopies. Correspondence (1935-37) concerning
  Miss Lenski's doll and toy collection, books for children,
  and her additions to the Lenski collection at the Milner
  Library at Illinois State Univ.; mss. of Miss Lenski's books,
  COAL CAMP GIRL (1959), CORN FARM BOY (1953), and HOUSEBOAT
  GIRL (1957); articles, plays, and speeches; bookmarks,
  Christmas cards and illustrations designed by Miss Lenski;
  photo albums, sketchbooks, scrapbooks and clippings, and a
  tape recording entitled, "A Talk with Lois Lenski." The
  bulk of the material relates to Miss Lenski's Regional Books
  and Round About America Books.

  misc. papers. original art
  In State Univ. of New York (Buffalo, N.Y.)
  For a description of this collection see THE LOIS LENSKI
  CHILDREN'S COLLECTION IN THE EDWARD H. BUTLER LIBRARY,

LENSKI, LOIS
  Caroline Giambra, 1972.
  Univ. also has 3 other collections donated by the author.

  misc. papers, 1927-63. 12 ft.
  In Syracuse Univ. Library (Syracuse, N.Y.)
  Notebooks, mss. of writings, galley sheets and page proof
  galleys, original and blueprint drawings, lithographs and
  illustrations, children's blocks designed by Miss Lenski.

  misc. papers. original art
  In Univ. of North Carolina Library (Greensboro, N.C.)

  misc. papers, 1893-1958. 3 ft.
  In Univ. of Oklahoma Library (Norman, Okla.)
  Correspondence, notes, mss. and galley proofs of books,
  brochures, drawings, and photos.

  misc. papers, 1937-70. ca. 200 items
  In Warder Public Library of Springfield and Clark County
  (Springfield, Ohio)
  Mss. of books, original drawings, printer's dummies, and
  personal photos.

LEVINGER, ELMA EHRLICH, 1887-1958 (A)
  misc. papers, 1912-58. 1.5 ft.
  In Univ. of Oregon Library (Eugene, Or.)
  Papers consist of mss. of plays, novels, poems, and short
  stories, most of them related to or based on Jewish history
  and folklore.

LEWIS, CLIVE STAPLES, 1898-1963 (A)
  papers. ca. 1,000 items
  In Wheaton College Library (Wheaton, Ill.)
  In part, transcripts and photocopies. Correspondence, mss.
  of writings, articles and other papers relating to Lewis and
  his "circle" of authors; address by Owen Barfield entitled
  "C. S. Lewis," the libretto for the opera LILITH (1895), by
  George MacDonald, pictures relating to THE LORD OF THE RINGS
  (1954), by J. R. R. Tolkien, newspaper clippings, and other
  papers. Some of the papers relate to Owen Barfield, George
  MacDonald, and Dorothy Sayers. Lewis' correspondents include
  Mrs. Vera Gebbert, Dom Bede Griffiths, and Dr. C. S. Kilby.

LONDON, JACK, 1876-1916 (A)
  papers, 1888-1932. ca. 15,000 items
  In Henry E. Huntington Library (San Marino, Calif.)
  Personal and professional papers belonging to Jack and
  Charmian London and the Jack London estate. Includes the mss.
  of most of London's works.

LONDON, JACK
  misc. papers
  In Oakland Public Library (Oakland, Calif.)

  misc. papers
  In San Francisco Public Library (San Francisco, Calif.)

  misc. papers, 1897-1916. 182 items
  In Stanford Univ. Libraries (Stanford, Calif.)
  Chiefly letters by London to Mabel and Edward Applegarth and
  to his agent in London, James B. Pinker; 2 notes by London;
  mss. of 2 novels; 6 poems by London, and 5 poems by Edward
  Applegarth.

  misc. papers. photographs
  In Utah State Univ. Library (Logan, Utah)

LOTHROP, HARRIET MULFORD, 1844-1924 (A)
  misc. papers. photographs
  In Concord Free Public Library (Concord, Mass.)

LOTHROP FAMILY
  misc. papers, 1854-1959. ca. 175 items
  In Boston Public Library (Boston, Mass.)
  Correspondence, chiefly of Harriet Mulford (Stone) Lothrop
  (pseud. Margaret Sidney), relating to her literary career,
  and to her husband, Daniel Lothrop, and daughter, Margaret
  Mulford Lothrop.

LOVELACE, MAUD HART, 1892-   (A)
  papers, 1950-52
  In Univ. of Oregon Library (Eugene, Or.)
  Collection includes original illustrations for 2 of her books,
  BETSY AND THE GREAT WORLD (1952) and THE TUNE IS IN THE TREE
  (1950).

MCCALLUM, JOHN DENNIS, 1924-   (A)
  misc. papers, 1956-59. 6 items
  In Washington State Univ. Library (Pullman, Wash.)
  Mss., galley proofs and publisher's drafts of published works
  including THE TIGER WORE SPIKES (1956) and BEGINNER'S BOOK OF
  FISHING (1958).

MCCLOSKEY, ROBERT (A,I)
  original art. 537 items
  In Emporia State Univ. Library, May Massee Collection
  (Emporia, Kan.)
  Misc. artwork for: TRIGGER JOHN'S SON (1934), LENTIL (1940),
  MAKE WAY FOR DUCKLINGS (1941), THE MAN WHO LOST HIS HEAD
  (1942), HOMER PRICE (1943), BLUEBERRIES FOR SAL (1948),

MCCLOSKEY, ROBERT
   CENTERBURG TALES (1951), ONE MORNING IN MAINE (1952),
   JOURNEY CAKE, HO!(1953), JUNKET (1955), TIME OF WONDER
   (1957), HENRY REED, INC.(1958), BURT DOW (1963), HENRY
   REED'S JOURNEY (1963), HENRY REED'S BABY-SITTING SERVICE
   (1966).

MCCLURG, (A.C.) AND COMPANY
   records, 1878-1967. ca. 5,100 items
   In Newberry Library (Chicago, Ill.)
   Correspondence, contracts, royalty statements, record books,
   scrapbooks, and other papers (largely dated after 1940).
   Authors represented include Edgar Rice Burroughs and Zane
   Grey.

MCCORD, DAVID, 1897-   (poet)
   misc. papers
   In Harvard Univ., Houghton Library (Cambridge, Mass.)

MACDONALD, GEORGE, 1824-1905 (A)
   misc. papers
   In Wheaton College Library (Wheaton, Ill.)

MCGINLEY, PHYLLIS, 1905-1978 (poet)
   papers, 1924-63. 12 ft.
   In Syracuse Univ. Library (Syracuse, N.Y.)
   Correspondence, childhood novels and poems, work notebooks,
   drafts of Miss McGinley's books, galleys, worksheets, copies
   of poems, prose, and an untitled play, published poems,
   prose, reviews, and articles, mss. of reviews, photos, and
   other papers. Correspondents include American magazines
   and publishing houses, Charles Abbott, Franklin P. Adams,
   Richard Armour, W. H. Auden, Jacques Barzun, John Mason
   Brown, Cass Canfield, Katherine Cornell, Margaret Cousins,
   Rumer Godden, the Hayden family, Robert Hillyer, Jean Kerr,
   Sinclair Lewis, Russell Lynes, Mary Margaret McBride,
   Groucho Marx, Ogden Nash, Rex Stout, A. M. Sullivan, and
   Louis Untermeyer.

MCGIVERN, MAUREEN (DALY) 1921-   (A)
   papers, 1938-73. 6 ft.
   In Univ. of Oregon Library (Eugene, Or.)
   Personal and professional correspondence (chiefly with Dodd,
   Mead and Co.), literary mss., television scripts, printed
   matter, and memorabilia.

MCGRAW, ELOISE JARVIS, 1915-   (A)*
   papers, 1949-77. 18 ft.
   In Univ. of Oregon Library (Eugene, Or.)
   Correspondence, ms. of William McGraw's HORSE IN THE HOUSE

MCGRAW, ELOISE JARVIS
   (1964), and a copy of the book revised for British
   publication. Correspondents include Dorothy Starr and Alice
   Torrey, juvenile editors of Coward-McCann, Thomas R. Coward,
   and L. H. Jarvis. Includes correspondence between Alice
   Torrey and William McGraw.

MACHETANZ, SARA BURLESON, 1918-   (A)
   misc. papers, 1954-61. 1 folder
   In Univ. of Oregon Library (Eugene, Or.)
   Includes 40 letters and diary, 1954-55, written at Unalakeet,
   Alaska.

MCINTOSH, GERALD J., 1894-   (collector)
   dime novel collection, 1879-1967. 12 ft.
   In Univ. of Arkansas Library (Fayetteville, Ark.)
   Correspondence, notes, memoranda, lists, printed matter, and
   other material relating to the history of the American dime
   novel and to McIntosh's interests and activities in the field.
   Includes complete files of Street & Smith's periodicals,
   TIP TOP WEEKLY and NEW TIP TOP WEEKLY for the years 1896-
   1915, with McIntosh's extensive marginalia and ms. material
   laid in.

MACKINSTRY, ELIZABETH (A,I)
   original art. 2 items
   In Emporia State Univ. Library, May Massee Collection
   (Emporia, Kan.)
   Misc. artwork for: THE FAIRY ALPHABET (1933).

MCLELLAND, ISABEL COUPER (A)
   misc. papers, 1941-62. ca. 2 ft.
   In Univ. of Oregon Library (Eugene, Or.)
   Correspondence with Henry Holt and Co., with readers and
   librarians; and mss. of 4 juvenile books.

MACMANUS, GEORGE, 1884-1954 (I)
   misc. papers
   In Univ. of California Libraries (Los Angeles, Calif.)
   Collection includes drawings, proofs and scrapbooks.

MANSFIELD, NORMA BICKNELL, 1906-1965 (A)
MANSFIELD, ROBERT STUART, 1929-1960 (A)
   papers of Norma B. and Robert Stuart Mansfield, 1929-60.
   ca. 5 ft.
   In Univ. of Oregon Library (Eugene, Or.)
   Correspondence and literary mss. of Mrs. Mansfield and her
   husband. Correspondents include Brandt and Brandt (literary
   agency), Edwin B. Chappell, Jr. (Dept. of Sunday Schools,
   Methodist Episcopal Church, South), Rowena Ferguson (Board of

MANSFIELD, NORMA BICKNELL
MANSFIELD, ROBERT STUART
   Christian Education, Methodist Episcopal Church, South),
   Elizabeth L. Gilman (Farrar & Rinehart), Anne Stoddard
   (American Girl editor), and other editors and publishers.

MARSHALL, JAMES, 1942-   (A,I)*
   misc. papers. 6 in.
   In Univ. of Oregon Library (Eugene, Or.)
   Collection includes 3 sketchbooks, a holograph manuscript of
   YUMMERS (1972), with original ink drawings, correspondence
   and copies of 6 of the author's books.

MASON, ARTHUR, 1876-1955 (A)
MASON, MARY (FRANKS), 1888-1966 (A)
   misc. papers, 1919-66. ca. 2 ft.
   In Univ. of Oregon Library (Eugene, Or.)
   Correspondence with agents and publishers, mss. of novels and
   short stories, contracts and reviews. Papers consist of
   correspondence with publishers and friends, mss. of children's
   stories and articles on children's literature and library
   service. Correspondents include Elmer Hader, Edwin Muir,
   Elmer Rice, and Sherwood Trask.

MASSEE, MAY, 1883-1966 (editor)
   misc. papers, 1923-63
   In Emporia State Univ., William Allen White Library
   (Emporia, Kan.)
   Correspondence, photographs and related material from her
   years as editor at Doubleday, Page and Co., and Viking Press.

MAY, CHARLES PAUL, 1920-   (A)*
   misc. papers, 1961-67. 1 box
   In Univ. of Oregon Library (Eugene, Or.)
   Papers include book mss., published items, and correspondence
   with Macmillan and Co., publisher.

MELTZER, MILTON, 1915-   (A)
   papers, 1956-75. 15 ft.
   In Univ. of Oregon Library (Eugene, Or.)
   Papers consist of books mss. in various stages, notes, and
   correspondence with subjects and informants. Correspondents
   include Langston Hughes, Arna Bontemps, and C. Eric Lincoln.

METHODIST BOOK CONCERN
   record, 1796-1911. 72 items. 2 v. and 2 folders
   In Methodist Publishing House Library (Nashville, Tenn.)
   Records (1796-1896) taken from the General Conference of the
   Methodist Episcopal Church; correspondence, financial reports,
   minutes of meetings, record of purchases, lists of mss. and
   of German publications, mss. of articles sent to the Western

METHODIST BOOK CONCERN
    Christian Advocate, and other records (1867-1911) from the
    Western Section of the Methodist Book Concern.

METHODIST PUBLISHING HOUSE
    misc. records, 1776-1936. ca. 90 items and 14 v.
    In Methodist Publishing House Library (Nashville, Tenn.)
    Correspondence, reports, journals, sermons, addresses, church
    register, minutes of meetings, clippings and other papers.

MILHOUS, KATHERINE, 1894-1977 (A,I)*
    misc. papers, 1938-64. 176 items
    In Free Library of Philadelphia (Philadelphia, Pa.)
    Misc. artwork and related material for: ONCE UPON A TIME
    (1938), CORPORAL KEEPERUPPER (1943), APPOLONIA'S VALENTINE
    (1954), THROUGH THESE ARCHES (1964).

MILLER, BERTHA MAHONY (editor)
    misc. papers. 27 items
    In Emporia State Univ. Library, May Massee Collection
    (Emporia, Kan.)

MONATH, ELIZABETH (A,I)
    original art. 22 items
    In Emporia State Univ. Library, May Massee Collection
    (Emporia, Kan.)
    Misc. artwork for: TOPPER AND THE GIANTS (1960)

MONTGOMERY, MAX
    pseud. see ATWATER, MONTGOMERY MEIGS

MONTGOMERY, RUTHERFORD GEORGE, 1894-   (A)
    papers, 1930-74. 20 ft. including 6,000 letters
    In Univ. of Oregon Library (Eugene, Or.)
    Correspondence and mss. of juvenile novels, short stories and
    film scripts. Correspondents include Jack Bates Abbott,
    Caxton Printers, Doubleday and Co., Henry Holt & Co.,
    Lenniger Literary Agency, David McKay Co., Joseph T. Shaw
    (agent), and Willis K. Wing (agent).

MOORE, ANNE CARROLL, 1871-1961 (A)
    papers, ca. 1900-60. 6 boxes
    In New York Public Library (N.Y.)
    Letters from authors, illustrators, publishers, friends, etc.
    relating to Miss Moore's books, especially NICHOLAS AND THE
    GOLDEN GOOSE (1932) and THE ART OF BEATRIX POTTER (1955),
    with some layout material and other miscellany.
    Correspondents inlcude Rhoda Brooks Balfour, Margery Bianco,
    L. Leslie Brooke, Sybil D. Brooke, James H. Daugherty,
    Walter de la Mare, Eleanor Farjeon, Dorothy Canfield Fisher,

MOORE, ANNE CARROLL
   Beatrix Potter and Carl Sandburg.

MOORE, LILLIAN (A)
   misc. papers, 1959-68. ca. 2 ft.
   In Univ. of Oregon Library (Eugene, Or.)
   Mss. of 6 books together with 20 published items.

MOORE, ROSALIE, 1910-   (A)
   papers, 1935-70. 1.5 ft. 437 letters
   In Univ. of Oregon Library (Eugene, Or.)
   Includes galley proofs, tear sheets, magazines and reviews.
   Correspondents include John Ciardi, Karl Shapiro, Louis
   Untermeyer.

MOREY, WALTER, 1907-   (A)
   papers, 1938-65. 5 ft.
   In Univ. of Oregon Library (Eugene, Or.)
   Correspondence with the Lenniger Literary Agency and mss. of
   Morey's books, GENTLE BEN (1965), HOME IS THE NORTH (1967),
   and SILVER HARVEST, and 14 short stories and articles.

MOWAT, FARLEY, 1921-   (A)
   papers
   In McMaster Univ. Library (Hamilton, Ont.)
   Collection contains correspondence and research files as well
   as mss. of published works

MUDGE, ISADORE GILBERT, 1875-1957 (librarian)
   misc. papers, 1914-41. ca. 4,000 items
   In Columbia Univ., Butler Library (N.Y.)
   Correspondence with librarians and bookdealers relating to
   Miss Mudge's collection of children's periodicals and card
   file (3,500) index of magazine titles.

MUELLER, HANS ALEXANDER (I)*
   original art. 4 items
   In Emporia State Univ. Library, May Massee Collection
   (Emporia, Kan.)
   Misc. artwork for: SON OF THE DANUBE (1940).

MUNROE, KIRK, 1850-1930 (A)
   papers. ca. 2,500 items
   In Library of Congress, Manuscript Division (Washington, D.C.)
   Correspondence; diaries, handwritten drafts and printed
   copies of books, short stories, essays, poetry and articles;
   biographical material, scrapbooks, subject files, an
   autograph book, newspaper clippings, printed matter, photos,
   drawings, and memorabilia. The bulk of the collection relates
   to Munroe's literary career, his adventures on a survey team

MUNROE, KIRK
    for the Union Pacific Railroad and the Atchison, Topeka and
    Santa Fe Railway; his trips into the Everglades and the
    Hudson Bay Region and to the Far East on a world tour; his
    work on behalf of the Seminole Indians of Florida; and his
    canoeing and bicycling interests. Includes correspondence
    of Munroe's second wife, Mabel (Stearns) Munroe, with
    reference to a proposed biography of Munroe.

NAST, THOMAS, 1840-1902 (cartoonist)
    original art. 65 items
    In Boston Public Library, Print Collection (Boston, Mass.)

    misc. papers. original art
    In MacCulloch Hall (Morristown, N.J.)
    Ca. 170 original works of art, 140 misc. photographs, 72
    pieces of correspondence and holograph notes. Artwork includes
    preliminary drawings, pen and ink sketches, proofs of wood
    engravings, paintings, a "9' X 12' charicaturama" (water
    color on muslin. Correspondence mainly from Nast to members
    of his family during his year's service as U. S. Ambassador
    to Ecuador. Many of the letters are illustrated with pen
    and ink sketches.

    misc. papers, 1860-1902. 6 boxes
    In Rutherford B. Hayes Library (Fremont, Ohio)
    Correspondence, diary (1860-61), literary mss., account
    book (1860), scrapbooks, notebook, sketches, caricatures,
    clippings, photos., portraits, designs, and miscellaneous
    printed matter.

    original art
    In Univ. of Kansas, Albert T. Reid Cartoon Collection
    (Lawrence, Kan.)

NATHAN, DOROTHY GOLDEEN (A)
    misc. papers, 1961-66. 1 box
    In Univ. of Oregon Library (Eugene, Or.)
    Correspondence with Miss Nathan's publisher Random House and
    with readers concerning her books WOMEN OF COURAGE (1964) and
    THE SHY ONE (1966).

NEWBERRY, CLARE TURLAY, 1903-1970 (A,I)*
    misc. papers, original art, 1910-69. 3 ft.
    In Univ. of Oregon Library (Eugene, Or.)
    Collection includes 242 original drawings, sketches and
    illustrations, 3 book dummies, and scrapbooks from childhood
    and early school years.

NORTH, STERLING, 1906-1974 (A)
   misc. papers, 1952-64. ca. 1 ft.
   In Boston Univ. Library (Boston, Mass.)
   Correspondence, mss. of writings, financial records, and
   other items concerning the publication of North's works
   beginning with his book ABE LINCOLN, LOG CABIN TO WHITE
   HOUSE (1956).

O'DELL, SCOTT, 1903-   (A)
   misc. papers, 1960. 1 item
   In Free Library of Philadelphia (Philadelphia, Pa.)
   Typescript of ISLAND OF THE BLUE DOLPHINS (1960).

   misc. papers. 1 ft.
   In Univ. of Oregon Library (Eugene, Or.)
   Collection comprises manuscript of and correspondence
   concerning THE CRUISE OF THE ARCTIC STAR (1973).

OGLE, LUCILLE (editor)
   papers and library. 40 ft. and 3,500 v.
   In Univ. of Oregon Library (Eugene, Or.)
   Papers include correspondence, mss., galleys, layouts,
   dummies, original illustrations given to Miss Ogle. Library
   includes work collected for possible use by or as produced by
   her publishers, Artists and Writers Guild, Simon and Schuster,
   Herder Co., Golden Press (Western Printing).

O'MORE PEGGY
   pseud. see BLOCKLINGER, PEGGY O'MORE

PAGE, THOMAS NELSON, 1853-1922 (A)
   misc. papers, 1893-1953. 305 items
   In College of William and Mary Library (Williamsburg, Va.)
   Correspondence, of Page, of his wife, Florence Lathrop Field
   Page, and of their daughters, Minna (Page)Burnaby and
   Florence (Page) Lindsay. Includes letters from Rome while
   Page was U. S. Ambassador to Italy, 1913-19.

   papers, 1739-1926. 9,276 items and 2 v.
   In Duke Univ. Library (Durham, N.C.)
   Correspondence, legal and business papers, diplomatic
   dispatches and other items (chiefly 1885-1920) relating to
   Page's legal and literary career, his activities as a lyceum
   lecturer, his marriages, and his interest in civic affairs,
   social reform, race relations, politics, and European travel.
   Includes family correspondence of Page and his brother,
   Rosewell Page, and his mother, Elizabeth Burwell Nelson Page;
   letters (before 1880) of various other members of the Page
   family. Described in GUIDE TO THE MANUSCRIPT COLLECTIONS IN
   THE DUKE UNIVERSITY LIBRARY, by N. M. Tilley and N. L. Goodwin
   (1947).

PAGE, THOMAS NELSON
misc. papers
In Univ. of Virginia Library, Clifton Waller Barrett
Collection (Charlottesville, Va.)

PAINE, ALBERT BIGELOW, 1861-1937 (A)
misc. papers, 1918-37. ca. 100 items
In American Academy of Arts and Letters Library (N.Y.)
Correspondence chiefly relating to the National Institute of
Arts and Letters, together with ca. 30 letters from public
figures in France. Names prominently mentioned are Marshall
Foch, Myron Timothy Herrick, Edward House, Jean Adrien Antoine
Jules Jusserand, Raymond Poincare, and Mark Twain.

misc. papers, 1890-1934. ca. 1,950 items
In Henry E. Huntington Library (San Marino, Calif.)

PARRISH, MAXFIELD, 1870-1966 (I)
misc. papers. original art
In Free Library of Philadelphia (Philadelphia, Pa.)

misc. papers, 1888-1950. ca. 60 items
In Haverford College Library, Quaker Collection (Haverford,
Pa.)
Letters, drawings, printed articles about Parrish, and
reproductions of his work. Includes 13 letters (1891-1954)
concerning Haverford College affairs; sketches for Haverford
College alumni reunions and a classbook; and sketches in a
German reader and chemistry and physics notebooks used by
Parrish at Haverford College (1888-91).

PAULL, GRACE A. (A,I)*
original art. 70 items
In Emporia State Univ. Library, May Massee Collection
(Emporia, Kan.)
Misc. artwork for: PANCAKES FOR BREAKFAST (1939), HOMESPUN
PLAYDAYS (1941), COUNTRY-STOP (1942), PIONEER ART IN
AMERICA (1944), AUGUSTUS (1945).

PERKINS, LUCY FITCH, 1865-1937 (A)
misc. papers, 1910. 10 items
In Free Library of Philadelphia (Philadelphia, Pa.)
Manuscript in pencil of DUTCH TWINS (1910).

PETERSHAM, MAUD (FULLER), 1889-1971 (A,I)*
PETERSHAM, MISKA, 1889-1960 (A,I)*
original art. 14 items
In Emporia State Univ. Library, May Massee Collection
(Emporia, Kan.)
Misc. artwork for: POPPY SEED CAKES (1924), MIKI (1929),

PETERSHAM, MAUD (FULLER)
PETERSHAM, MISKA
  THE CHRIST CHILD (1931), GET-A-WAY AND HÁRY JÁNOS (1933),
  MIKI AND MARY (1934).

  misc. papers, 1930-58. 1 box
  In Univ. of Oregon Library (Eugene, Or.)
  Drawings, watercolors, crayon illustrations, proofs, book
  dummies, and a book manuscript for 18 books.

PETRY, ANN (LANE), 1911-   (A)
  papers, 1940-68. 150 items
  In Boston Univ. Library (Boston, Mass.)
  Correspondence, Mrs. Petry's writings in variant drafts,
  galleys, and memorabilia.
  Additions to the collection are anticipated.

PIKE, JAMES, 1777-1842 (editor)
  papers, 1793-1842. 1 ft.
  In Syracuse Univ. Library (Syracuse, N.Y.)
  Correspondence, diaries, legal papers, commonplaces, ms.
  school materials, and miscellaneous writings relating to
  Pike's teaching and writing career, and to the printing and
  publishing of his books in New England, especially Me. and
  Mass. Names represented include Etheridge & Bliss, Daniel
  Johnson, Nathan Kinsman, Nicholas Pike, and the Pike family.

PINKERTON, ROBERT EUGENE, 1882-1970 (A)
PINKERTON, KATHRENE SUTHERLAND (A)
  papers. 5 ft.
  In Univ. of Oregon Library (Eugene, Or.)
  Wrote fiction and articles with outdoor and adventure themes,
  much of their early work appearing in pulp magazines. Papers
  consist of mss. of books, short stories, and articles, as well
  as printed pieces. Correspondence includes 14 letters, 1936-
  40 from Stewart Edward White.

PITZ, HENRY CLARENCE, 1895-1976 (A,I)*
  papers, 1927-67. 10 ft.
  In Univ. of Oregon Library (Eugene, Or.)
  Correspondence (1,374 letters) with writers, publishers, and
  artists, mss. of 5 books, 335 original illustrations, 69 in
  color; 42 etchings and lithographs, and 32 books illustrated
  by Pitz.

PLOWHEAD, RUTH GIPSON, 1877-1970 (A)
  misc. papers, 1931-69. 3 ft.
  In Univ. of Oregon Library (Eugene, Or.)
  Minor correspondence, mss. of short stories and mss. of books
  with original illustrations by Agnes Randall Moore.

60

POGANY, WILLY, 1882-1955 (I)
  original art, 1913-54. 500 pieces
  In Univ. of Oregon Library (Eugene, Or.)
  Original drawings, sketches, etchings, watercolors, and oils
  done for newspapers, magazines and books.

POTTER, BEATRIX, 1866-1943 (A,I)*
  misc. papers, original art, 1885-1943. 237 items
  In Free Library of Philadelphia (Philadelphia, Pa.)
  Correspondence, mss. of Miss Potter's THE TAILOR OF
  GLOUCESTER (1901) and THE TALE OF LITTLE PIG ROBINSON (1930),
  paintings and pen-and-ink drawings for these works together
  with 100 from her own portfolio, 29 inscribed copies of her
  books, and other papers relating to her career.
  Correspondents include Mrs. James DeWolf Perry and Miss
  Potter's American publisher, David McKay Co.

PRICE, CHRISTINE, 1928-   (A,I)*
  papers, original art, 1948-76. 6 ft.
  In Univ. of Oregon Library (Eugene, Or.)
  Collection consists of over 1,000 original illustrations for
  20 books and mss. of 6 books by Miss Price.

PRICE, MARGARET EVANS, 1888-1973 (A,I)
  misc. papers. 1 ft.
  In Univ. of Oregon Library (Eugene, Or.)
  Collection includes original artwork for THE WINDY SHORE, A
  TALE OF OLD MARSEILLES (1930) and other unidentified works.
  Some copies of her books included.

PYLE, HOWARD, 1853-1911 (I)
  original art
  In Delaware Art Museum Library (Wilmington, Del.)
  Also includes files of secondary material and a portion of
  Pyle's personal library.

  misc. papers. original art
  In Free Library of Philadelphia, Rare Book Dept.
  (Philadelphia, Pa.)

RACKHAM, ARTHUR, 1867-1939 (A)
  misc. papers, original art, 1904-67. ca. 600 items
  In Columbia Univ., Butler Library (N.Y.)
  Letters written by Rackham; Christmas cards of his design;
  notebooks, mss., and proofs for Derek Hudson's: ARTHUR
  RACKHAM : HIS LIFE AND WORK (1960); and other papers
  relating to Rackham.

  misc. papers, original art, 1893-1938. 65 items
  In Free Library of Philadelphia (Phialdelphia, Pa.)
  Correspondence addressed mainly to Frank P. Harris, sketches,

61

RACKHAM, ARTHUR
  drawings, paintings, and other papers relating to Rackham's
  career as illustrator of books, articles and periodicals.

  misc. papers. original art
  In Univ. of Louisville Library (Louisville, Ky.)

RAWLINGS, MARJORIE (KINNAN), 1896-1953 (A)
  misc. papers, 1916-53. ca. 300 items
  In Univ. of Florida Libraries (Gainesville, Fla.)
  In part, transcritps (typewritten), photocopies (positive),
  and microfilm (negative). Correspondence, including over 200
  letters from Maxwell Perkins, 33 from Sigrid Undset, 25 from
  Archibald Joseph Cronin, 43 from James Branch Cabell, and
  others; early drafts of novels, short stories and speeches;
  notes and typewritten copies of letters collected by Mrs.
  Rawlings for a projected biography of Ellen Glasgow;
  scrapbooks, newspaper clippings, and photos. Bulk of material
  covers the period 1930-53.

RECK, FRANKLIN MERING, 1896-1965 (A)
  papers, 1921-65. 4 ft.
  In Univ. of Oregon Library (Eugene, Or.)
  Personal and professional correspondence, including letters
  (1921-24) from Iowa Agricultural College, and mss. of stories
  for boys.

RICHARDS, LAURA E., 1850-1943 (A)
  misc. papers
  In Colby College Library (Waterville, Me.)
  Correspondence between Laura Richards and Edward Arlington
  Robinson.

  misc. papers
  In Gardiner Public Library (Gardiner, Me.)
  Collection includes manuscript for CAPTIAN JANUARY (1891),
  miscellaneous correspondence, manuscript poems, photographs
  and newspaper clippings.

RIDEING, WILLIAM HENRY, 1853-1918 (editor)
  misc. papers, 1894-1918. 259 items
  In Boston Public Library (Boston, Mass.)
  One time editor of YOUTH'S COMPANION. Letters from Rideing
  to William Morris Colles (1855-1926), English editor and
  literary agent, concerning the marketing of literary
  properties.

RIDLE, JULIA BROWN, 1923- (A)
  misc. papers. 2 items
  In Washington State Univ. Library (Pullman, Wash.)
  Mss. drafts of novel, HOG WILD! (1961)

RIETVELD, JANE (A,I)
  original art. 123 items
  In Emporia State Univ. Library, May Massee Collection
  (Emporia, Kan.)
  Misc. artwork for: NICKY'S BUGLE (1947), GREAT LAKES SAILOR
  (1952), ROLY AND POLY (1956), MONKEY ISLAND (1963).

RILEY, JAMES WHITCOMB, 1849-1916 (poet)
  misc. papers, 1888-1916. ca. 50 items
  In American Academy of Arts and Letters Library (N.Y.)
  Correspondence, chiefly relating to the American Academy of
  Arts and Letters, and mss. of various poems by Riley.

  misc. papers, ca. 1879-1904. ca. 140 items
  In Henry E. Huntington Library (San Marino, Calif.)
  Correspondence and literary mss. Includes 55 letters to
  William Carey. Other correspondents include Bliss Carman,
  Madison Cawein, and Charles Warren Stoddard.

  papers, 1858-1944. 6,245 items
  In Indiana Univ., Lilly Library (Bloomington, Ind.)
  Collection contains: correspondence, drafts, fair copies and
  typescripts of poems; pen and pencil drawings by Riley and
  two patent medicine signs painted by Riley. Correspondents
  include George Ade, Clara Louise Bottsford, Elizabeth Kahle
  Brunn, Robert Jones Burdette, Frances Eliza (Hodgson) Burnett,
  George Washington Cable, Bliss Carman, Mary (Hartwell)
  Catherwood, Madison Julius Cawein, John Marcus Dickey, Eugene
  Field, Zona Gale, Hamlin Garland, Lee O. Harris, William M.
  Herschell, George C. Hitt, Charles Louis Holstein, Oliver
  Wendell Holmes, Robert Underwood Johnson, George Washington
  Julian, Clara Elizabeth Laughlin, George Barr McCutcheon,
  John Tinney McCutcheon, Edith Thomas Medairy, Silar Weir
  Mitchell, Louise (Chandler) Moulton, Meredith Nicolson,
  Edgar Wilson Nye, Walter Hines Page, John Sanburn Phillips,
  John Clark Ridpath, Kate Douglas (Smith) Wiggin Riggs,
  Theodore Clement Stells, Frank Richard Stockton, Booth
  Tarkington, Maurice Thompson, Clara Vawter, Ella (Wheeler)
  Wilcox, among many others.
  Note: Extensive mss. of Riley material is held by the Lilly
  Library in the following collections: Clara Louise Bottsford
  mss. (350 items); Elizabeth D. Brunn mss. (46 items);
  Callahan family mss. (4 items); John Marcus Dickey mss. (2,161
  items); Charles Louis Holstein mss. (124 items)

RILEY-EITEL PAPERS
  misc. papers, 1870-1920. ca. 12 boxes and 2 file drawers
  In Indianapolis Public Library (Indianapolis, Ind.)
  In part, transcripts (typewritten); correspondence, a few mss.,
  poems, a history and other papers of the Riley family, and

RILEY-EITEL PAPERS
photos. Includes correspondence and other papers of Riley's
nephew, Edmund H. Eitel, some of which are related to Riley;
many copies of Riley's letters and poems made by or for Eitel
for a proposed biography. Correspondents include Robert J.
Burdette, Bliss Carman, Edgar Wilson Nye, William Lyon
Phelps, John Riley, and other members of the Riley family.

RIPLEY, ELIZABETH BLAKE, 1906-1969 (A)
    misc. papers, 1966-68. 189 items
    In Free Library of Philadelphia (Philadelphia, Pa.)
    Mss. and related material for: RODIN : A BIOGRAPHY (1966),
    HOKUSAI (1968).

ROBINSON, LINCOLN FAY (A,I)
    original art. 58 items
    In Emporia State Univ. Library, May Massee Collection
    (Emporia, Kan.)
    Misc. artwork for: TWO BOYS (1932)

ROBINSON, MABEL LOUISE, 1882?-1962 (A)
    papers, ca. 1930-59. 20 boxes
    In Columbia Univ., Butler Library (N.Y.)
    Professor of juvenile literature at Columbia Univ.
    Correspondence relating primarily to publication of Miss
    Robinson's novels and short stories, mss. of writings, lecture
    notes, business papers, photos, memorabilia, and clippings
    and reprints. Includes typescripts and drafts of the
    following works: RUNNER OF THE MOUNTAIN TOP (1939), ISLAND
    NOON (1942), BITTER FORFEIT (1947), THE DEEPENING YEAR (1950),
    STRONG WINDS (1951), SKIPPER RILEY (1955).

ROJANKOVSKY, FEODOR, 1891-   (I)*
    original art. 1 item
    In Emporia State Univ. Library, May Massee Collection
    (Emporia, Kan.)
    Misc. artwork for: THE TREASURE TROVE OF THE SUN (1952).

ROOT, MARY ELIZABETH (STAFFORD), 1868-1953 (librarian)
    papers, 1892-1953. 3 ft.
    In Rhode Island Historical Society (Providence, R.I.)
    Personal and business correspondence, autobiography, articles,
    lectures, and clippings, chiefly 1913-22, relating to
    children's libraries and reading.

RUTLAND, EVA (A)
    papers, 1952-69. 1 box including 131 letters
    In Univ. of Oregon Library (Eugene, Or.)
    Papers consist of mss. of children's books and personal and
    professional correspondence. Major correspondents are
    Abingdon Press and Lenniger Literary Agency.

SANDOZ, MARI SUSETTE, 1896-1966 (A)
  papers, 1934-66. ca. 1,000 items
  In Nebraska State Historical Society (Lincoln, Neb.)
  Correspondence, biographical and historical sketches of
  western Neb., magazine articles by Miss Sandoz, clippings of
  book reviews, notices for her books, including OLD JULES
  (1935) and SLOGUM HOUSE (1937), biographical sketches of Miss
  Sandoz, and factual and fictional stories about the West and
  Indian tribes. Includes letters relating to the writing and
  publication of Miss Sandoz's books. Correspondents include
  Jay Amos Barrett, Mamie Jane Meredith, and Addison E. Sheldon.

  misc. papers, 1925-66. ca. 200 ft.
  In Univ. of Nebraska Library (Lincoln, Neb.)
  Correspondence with publishers, writers, scholars, and friends,
  mss. of published books, research files relating to Western
  American and Indian history, newspaper clipping about Miss
  Sandoz and her published works, photos, and Miss Sandoz's
  personal library, including her published books and books with
  her marginal notes.

SAWYER, RUTH, 1880-1970 (A)
  misc. papers
  In College of Sainte Catherine, Sainte Catherine Library
  (St. Paul, Minn.)
  Letters, photographs, scrapbook, unpublished storyteller's
  notebook, original book illustrations by Robert McCloskey and
  Hugh Troy; recordings, filmstrip, typescripts, contracts,
  awards; unpublished bio-bibliography, 32 pages listing all
  known writings; books (various editions), magazine articles
  and serials, selections in anthologies, reviews.

SCHREIBER, GEORGES, 1904-   (A,I)*
  original art. 39 items
  In Emporia State Univ. Library, May Massee Collection
  (Emporia, Kan.)
  Misc. artwork for: BAMBINO THE CLOWN (1947), PANCAKES-PARIS
  (1947), PROFESSOR BULL'S UMBRELLA (1954).

SCHULTZ, JAMES WILLARD, 1859-1947 (A)
  papers, 1910-47. 4 ft.
  In Montana State Univ. Library (Bozeman, Mont.)
  Literary mss., personal papers, press notices, and pictures
  relating mainly to American Indians.

SCOVEL, FREDERICK GILMAN, 1902-   (A)
SCOVEL, MYRA SCOTT, 1930-69 (A)
  papers. 1.5 ft.
  In Univ. of Oregon Library (Eugene, Or.)
  Mrs. Scovel wrote several books for children based on her
  China and India experience, the best-known being the

SCOVEL, FREDERICK GILMAN
SCOVEL, MYRA SCOTT
  autobiographical THE CHINESE GINGER JARS (1962). There are
  also mss. and related material for 5 books for children by
  Mrs. Scovel.

SCRIBNER'S (CHARLES) SONS, NEW YORK
  archives, 1878-1960. 200 ft.
  In Princeton Univ. Library (Princeton, N.J.)
  Authors' correspondence and business files.

SCUDDER, HORACE ELISHA, 1838-1902 (A)
  papers. 200 items
  In Washington Univ. Library (St. Louis, Mo.)
  Correspondence relating to his work, writings and social
  engagements. Scudder's correspondents include Margaret
  Deland, Edward Everett Hale, Sarah Orne Jewett, James
  Russell Lowell, Silas Weir Mitchell, Alice Elvira Freeman
  Palmer, Agnes Repplier, Edmund Clarence Stedman, Marion E.
  Stockton, Hudson Stuck, John Townsend Trowbridge, John
  Greenleaf Whittier, and Kate Douglas Wiggin. Documents
  relating to James Fenimore Cooper also included.

SECKAR, ALVENA (A)
  papers, 1940-56. 2 boxes, 1 folder
  In West Virginia Univ. Library (Morgantown, W. Va.)
  Mss. including ZUSKA OF THE BURNING HILLS (1952), TRAPPED IN
  THE OLD MINE (1953), and MISKO (1956).

SELSAM, MILLICENT (ELLIS), 1912-   (A)
  misc. papers, 1955-63. 1 ft.
  In Univ. of Oregon Library (Eugene, Or.)
  Mss. and related material for 11 books and copies of 7 books.

SEREDY, KATE, 1899-1975 (A,I)
  original art. 508 items
  In Emporia State Univ. Library, May Massee Collection
  (Emporia, Kan.)
  Misc. artwork for: THE GOOD MASTER (1935), LISTENING (1936),
  THE WHITE STAG (1937), AN EAR FOR UNCLE EMIL (1939), THE
  SINGING TREE (1939), A TREE FOR PETER (1941), THE OPEN GATE
  (1943), THE CHESTRY OAK (1948), GYPSY (1951), LITTLE VIC
  (1951), FINNEGAN II (1953), PHILOMENA (1955), THE TENEMENT
  TREE (1959), A BRAND-NEW UNCLE (1961), LAZY TINKA (1962).

  original art. 1 drawer
  In Univ. of Oregon Library (Eugene, Or.)
  Collection includes illustrations for CADDIE WOODLAWN (1935)
  by Carol Ryrie Brink; pieces for several other books, plus 4
  pastel portrait sketches.

SETON, ANYA, 1916-   (A)
  papers, 1878-1967. 100 items
  In Boston Univ. Library (Boston, Mass.)
  Chiefly correspondence, including letters and other papers
  from Miss Seton's mother, Grace Gallatin Seton, and a few
  records of Miss Seton's father, Ernest Thompson Seton,
  memorabilia, and other papers.

SETON, ERNEST THOMPSON, 1860-1946 (A)
  misc. papers, 1905-46. 60 items
  In American Academy of Arts and Letters Library (N.Y.)
  Correspondence chiefly relating to the National Institute of
  Arts and Letters.

  misc. papers.
  In American Museum of Natural History (N.Y.)
  Original diaries (1879-1946)

  misc. papers. original art. 3,000 pieces
  In Ernest Thompson Seton Memorial Library and Museum
  (Cimarron, N.M.)

SEUSS, DR.
  pseud. see GEISEL, THEODORE SEUSS

SEWELL, HELEN, 1896-1957 (I)*
  original art. 8 items
  In Emporia State Univ. Library, May Massee Collection
  (Emporia, Kan.)
  Misc. artwork for: BLUEBONNETS FOR LUCINDA (1934), THE YOUNG
  BRONTËS (1938).

SHACKELFORD, SHELBY, 1899-   (A,I)
  papers, 1936-43. 2 ft.
  In Univ. of Oregon Library (Eugene, Or.)
  Includes mss. and original artwork.

SHAHN, BEN, 1898-1969 (I)
  papers, 1929-62. 6 reels of microfilm. ca. 6,000 items
  In Archives of American Art (N.Y.)
  Microfilm made in 1963 from originals owned by Mr. Shahn.
  Correspondence, clippings, photos, and miscellaneous
  publications. Chiefly letters written to Shahn in the 1940's
  and 50's. Much of the correspondence is from publishers,
  dealers, museums, schools, corporations, and art organizations.
  Includes letters from Shahn's biographers, Selden Rodman and
  James Thrall Soby. Other correspondents include Leonard
  Baskin, Alexander Calder, Diego Rivera, Raphael Soyer, and
  William Carlos Williams.

SHURA, MARY FRANCIS
     pseud. see CRAIG, MARY FRANCIS

SIDNEY, MARGARET
     pseud. see LOTHROP, HARRIET MULFORD

SIGOURNEY, LYDIA HOWARD (HUNTLEY), 1791-1865 (A)
     misc. papers, 1830-62. 67 items
     In Columbia Univ., Butler Library (N.Y.)
     Letters from Mrs. Sigourney to her close friend, Mrs. Mary
     A. Patrick, daughter of Theodore Dwight, discussing personal,
     social, family, and literary subjects.

     misc. papers
     In Connecticut College Library (New London, Conn.)

     misc papers. ca. 100 items
     In Connecticut Historical Society (Hartford, Conn.)
     Letters of Mrs. Sigourney and of her husband, Charles
     Sigourney.

     misc. papers, 1832-65. 75 items
     In Trinity College Library (Hartford, Cónn.)
     Correspondence; ms. of Mrs. Sigourney's book, HISTORY OF
     MARCUS AURELIUS (1836); several sheets of poetry, some
     printed; daguerreotypes, and clippings.

     misc. papers
     In Univ. of Chicago Libraries (Chicago, Ill.)

     misc. papers
     In Univ. of Virginia, Alderman Library (Charlottesville, Va.)

     misc. papers
     In Yale Univ., Beinecke Library (New Haven, Conn.)

SIMON, HOWARD, 1903-   (I)
SIMON, MINA LEWITON (I)
     papers, 1954-67. 4 ft.
     In Univ. of Oregon Library (Eugene, Or.)
     Papers include original mss., dummies and artwork.

SINGER, ISAAC BASHEVIS, 1904-   (A)
     misc. papers, ca. 1960-67. 4 boxes
     In Columbia Univ., Butler Library (N.Y.)
     Mss., drafts and proofs of Mr. Singer's writings.

SINGMASTER, ELSIE, 1879-1958 (A)
     misc. papers. ca. 2 ft.
     In Adams County Historical Society (Gettysburg, Pa.)
     Correspondence, newspaper items, and other papers relating to

SINGMASTER, ELSIE
  Thaddeus Stevens.

SLOBODKIN, LOUIS, 1903-1975 (A,I)*
  papers. 8 ft. 7 boxes
  In Univ. of Oregon Library (Eugene, Or.)
  Collection includes correspondence, sketches, drawings,
  dummies, proofs, and mss., plus miscellaneous drawings,
  articles and speeches; scripts for radio programs.

SMITH, JESSIE WILCOX, 1863-1935 (I)
  misc. papers. original art
  In Free Library of Philadelphia, Rare Book Dept.
  (Philadelphia, Pa.)

SMITH, WILLIAM J., 1918-   (poet)*
  papers, ca. 1924-68. ca. 1,030 items
  In Washington Univ. Libraries (St. Louis, Mo.)
  Correspondence, journals, worksheets, corrected typescripts,
  drafts, notebooks, galley proofs, publicity material, and
  miscellaneous papers relating to Smith's books of poetry,
  translations, and writings for children. Includes drafts of
  poems by Guy Daniels, Stephen Spender, and Allen Tate;
  drafts of addresses by Louise Bogan and Richard Wilbur, and
  some papers relating to Smith's teaching activities at
  Williams College (1951) and his association with Grove
  Press.

SOGLOW, OTTO, 1900-1975 (cartoonist)
  original art. ca. 300 items
  In Boston Univ. Library, Department of Special Collections
  (Boston, Mass.)
  Original pen and ink drawings of the syndicated comic strip,
  "The Little King" and other cartoons.

SPEARE, ELIZABETH GEORGE, 1908-   (A)
  papers, 1957-67. 3 boxes
  In Boston Univ. Library, Department of Special Collections
  (Boston, Mass.)
  Mss. of THE ICE GLENN (unpublished), CALICO CAPTIVE (1957),
  THE WITCH OF BLACKBIRD POND (1958), THE BRONZE BOW (1961),
  and LIFE IN COLONIAL AMERICA (1963); correspondence with
  Houghton Mifflin.

SPROAT, NANCY DENNIS, 1766-1826 (A)
  misc. papers
  In Boston Athenaeum (Boston, Mass.)
  Collection contains mss. and manuscript fragments for 6 of
  her juveniles.

STEFFEN, ALICE JACQUELINE, 1907-   (A)
   papers, 1956-66. ca. 3 ft.
   In Univ. of Oregon Library (Eugene, Or.)
   Papers include mss. of 7 books and correspondence with agents
   and publishers, particularly McIntosh and Otis, John Day,
   Hawthorne Books, P. J. Kenedy & Sons, and Macmillan.

STEFFEN, JACK
   pseud. see STEFFEN, ALICE

STEIN, HARVÉ, 1904-   (I)*
   misc. papers. original art. 1 case
   In Univ. of Oregon Library (Eugene, Or.)
   Collection contains correspondence and original illustrations
   for GALILEO AND THE MAGIC NUMBERS (1958) and THE FIRST BOOK OF
   THE CALIFORNIA GOLD RUSH (1962).

STEPHENS, CHARLES ASBURY, 1844-1931
   papers. 41 boxes
   In Bowdoin College Library (Brunswick, Me.)
   Mainly mss., some correspondence.

STERLING, DOROTHY, 1913-   (A)
   papers, 1938-78
   In Univ. of Oregon Library (Eugene, Or.)
   Collection contains correspondence, research materials, mss.
   for books and articles, plus an unpublished history of Time,
   Inc., with supporting manuscript and source material,
   1923-50.

STERNE, EMMA GELDERS, 1894-1971 (A)
   papers, 1927-67. 3 ft., including 631 letters
   In Univ. of Oregon Library (Eugene, Or.)
   Papers include mss. and related material for 11 books and 2
   plays. There is a report on a peace march to Washington,
   D. C. in 1963. Major correspondents are: Artists and Writers
   Guild, Inc., Artists and Writers Press, Inc., Alfred A.
   Knopf, Inc., Marjory Lacey-Baker, Edith Margolis, and Gilda
   Tommasi of Lenniger Literary Agency, Simon & Schuster, Inc.,
   H. N. Swanson, Inc. There is also a file of letters received
   by the author in 1967 when she was interned at the Santa
   Rita, Calif. Rehabilitation Center for participation in an
   anti-draft demonstration October 16, 1967.

STEVENSON, JANET, 1913-   (A)
   papers, 1929-74. 8 ft.
   In Univ. of Oregon Library (Eugene, Or.)
   Papers include mss. of short stories, articles, biographies,
   plays, teleplays and poems.

STEVENSON, ROBERT LOUIS, 1850-1894 (A)
  misc. papers
  In Harvard Univ. Library (Cambridge, Mass.)

  misc. papers, 1852-94. ca. 160 items
  In Henry E. Huntington Library (San Marino, Calif.)
  Correspondence, sketches, musical works, and other literary
  mss. Includes letters regarding Stevenson's illness and 42
  letters to Will H. Low.

  misc. papers, 1800-1970. 5 ft. ca. 350 items
  In Silverado Museum (St. Helena, Calif.)
  61 letters of Stevenson; mss. of writings, diaries and address
  books of Stevenson and his wife; 91 letters of his wife,
  Fanny Van de Grift Stevenson, many of them to Stevenson's
  mother; 45 letters of Isobel Osbourne Strong Field,
  25 of Lloyd Osbourne; letters of Stevenson's grandparents,
  and correspondence concerning Stevenson of his step-grandson,
  Austin Strong, and others.

  misc. papers
  In Univ. of California, William Andrews Clark Memorial
  Library (Los Angeles, Calif.)

  misc. papers
  In Yale Univ., Beinecke Library (New Haven, Conn.)

  STRONG, AUSTIN, 1881-1952
  papers, 1925-52. ca. 3,500 items
  In Columbia Univ., Butler Library (N.Y.)
  Correspondence; 31 diaries; literary mss., notes and costume
  and scenic designs for more than 70 of Strong's plays and
  related writings; commonplace books; scrapbooks containing
  notes, travel sketches, original drawings, and photos; and
  other papers. Includes material relating to Robert Louis
  Stevenson and photos and letters from Samoa of Strong's
  mother, Isobel Strong, Stevenson's stepdaughter.
  Correspondents include H. Granville Barker, Sir Herbert
  Beerbohn-Tree, John Galsworthy, Booth Tarkington, and
  Thornton Wilder.

STONG, PHILIP DUFFIELD, 1899-1957 (A)
  misc. papers, 1922-56. 151 items ·
  In Univ. of Iowa Libraries (Iowa City, Iowa)
  In part, photocopies of original letters owned by Mrs. Harvey
  H. Davis. Correspondence and drafts of works, printer's
  copies with revisions, galley and page proofs. Correspondents
  include Cyril Clemens, Harvey Henry Daivs, and John Towner
  Frederick.

STOWE, HARRIET ELIZABETH (BEECHER), 1811-1896 (A)
  misc. papers
  In Johns Hopkins Univ. Library (Baltimore, Md.)

  papers, ca. 1825-96. 239 items
  In The Stowe-Day Memorial Library and Historical Foundation
  (Hartford, Conn.)
  Letters by Mrs. Stowe to friends, relatives, and publishers
  during the course of her career while residing in
  Cincinnati, Ohio (1832-50), Brunswick, Me. (1852), Andover,
  Mass. (1853-64), Hartford, Conn. (1864-96), and from her
  winter home in Mandarin, Fla. (1868-85); journal of travels
  in Italy (1860); brief biographical account of her childhood,
  describing the death of her mother, Roxana (Foote) Beecher,
  wife of Lyman Beecher; draft for part of her novel, AGNES OF
  SORRENTO (1862); and mss. of articles, poems, and other
  writings.

  misc. papers
  In Univ. of California, Bancroft Library (Berkeley, Calif.)

  misc. papers
  In Univ. of Virginia Library (Charlottesville, Va.)

BEECHER FAMILY
  papers, 1850-1946. 3 boxes
  In Radcliffe College, Women's Archives (Cambridge, Mass.)
  Correspondence, diaries, and photos. of James C. Beecher
  (1828-1886), his wife, Frances (Johnson) Beecher Perkins
  (b. 1832) and their adopted twin daughters, Mary Frances
  Beecher (d. 1952) and Margaret (Beecher) Ward. Includes
  letters of Harriet Beecher Stowe, (1811-1896).

  papers, 1706-1953. 30,000 items
  In Yale Univ., Beinecke Library (New Haven, Conn.)
  Correspondence, sermons, travel accounts, diaries, newspaper
  clippings, and other papers of Henry Ward Beecher (1813-1887),
  clergyman and orator, and of other members of the Beecher
  family, including letters of Harriet Elizabeth (Beecher)
  Stowe (1811-1896), to her brother, as well as some other
  Stowe material.

STRATEMAYER SYNDICATE
  misc. papers. 6 in.
  In Univ. of Oregon Library (Eugene, Or.)
  Edward Stratemayer, 1862-1927, was an author and founded the
  Stratemayer Syndicate which produced adventure story series
  for children, e.g. as Nancy Drew, Hardy Boys, Tom Swift,
  Honey Bunch, and Bobbsey Twin series. He wrote under 65
  different pseudonyms. Harriet Stratemayer Adams, his daughter,
  1901-   , continued writing the series after his death and

STRATEMAYER SYNDICATE
became an owner and manager of the Syndicate. Collection
includes fan letters for the years 1928-29 and mss. of 3
books by Stratemayer and a book by Adams, THE DOUBLE JINX
MYSTERY of the Nancy Drew series.

STRONG, BARBARA NOLEN, 1902-   (A)
papers, 1967-73. 3 ft.
In Univ. of Oregon Library (Eugene, Or.)
Editor of STORY PARADE from 1936-54. Mss. and related
material for AFRICA IS PEOPLE (1967), FIRST BOOK OF
ETHIOPIA (1971), AFRICA IS THUNDER AND WONDER (1972), and
MEXICO IS PEOPLE (1973).

STURTZEL, HOWARD ALLISON, 1894-   (A)
misc. papers, 1956-65. 1 box
In Univ. of Oregon Library (Eugene, Or.)
Writes nature novels for young people in collaboration with
his wife, Jane Levington Sturtzel, under the names Jane and
Paul Annixter. Collection consists of mss. and drafts of
5 novels.

SUMMERS, JAMES LEVINGSTON, 1910-   (A)
papers, 1945-69. 12 ft.
In Univ. of Oregon Library (Eugene, Or.)
Correspondence, literary mss., and published pieces.
Correspondents include agents, Ruth Cantor, McIntosh and Otis,
and Constance Smith, and publishers Doubleday and Co., Junior
Literary Guild, David McKay, and Westminster Press.

SWAYNE, SAMUEL F (A,I)
SWAYNE, ZOA L. (A,I)
original art. 54 items
In Emporia State Univ. Library, May Massee Collection
(Emporia, Kan.)
Misc. artwork for: GREAT-GRANDFATHER IN THE HONEY TREE (1949)

TARKINGTON, BOOTH, 1869-1946 (A)
misc. papers, 1908-44. ca. 150 items
In American Academy of Arts and Letters Library (N.Y.)
Correspondence relating to the National Institute of Arts
and Letters Library, and a manuscript of A GREAT MAN'S WIFE.

misc. papers, 1921-23. 43 items.
In Columbia Univ., Butler Library (N.Y.)
Correspondence with Ira A. Hards regarding the production of
the plays, "Intimate Strangers" and "Magnolia." Includes
copies of telegrams sent by Hards, the director of the plays,
and by A. L. Erlanger, the producer.

TARKINGTON, BOOTH
  misc. papers
  In Cornell Univ. Library (Ithaca, N.Y.)

  papers. ca. 500 boxes
  In Princeton Univ. Library (Princeton, N.J.)
  Correspondence, mss. of Tarkington's writings, clippings and
  other printed items, photos., and memorabilia. Described
  in the PRINCETON UNIVERSITY LIBRARY CHRONICLE, 16:45-53,
  Winter, 1955.

TEE-VAN, HELEN DAMROSCH, 1893-   (A,I)
  papers, 1900-69. 6 ft.
  In Univ. of Oregon Library (Eugene, Or.)
  Papers include drawings from several scientific expeditions,
  original artwork from 13 published books and one unpublished
  book, sketches and watercolors of murals and dioramas, and
  26 sketch books, 1900-29.

TENGGREN, GUSTAF ADOLF, 1896-1963 (I)*
  misc. papers, 1930-63. 6 ft.
  In Univ. of Oregon Library (Eugene, Or.)
  Papers include dummies, sketches, layouts or story boards,
  roughs, and final illustrations for 10 books, as well as
  some manuscript material.

TERHUNE, ALBERT PAYSON, 1872-1942 (A)
  misc. papers, 1909-34. 75 items
  In Central Connecticut State College Library (New Britain,
  Conn.)
  Chiefly correspondence with William Gerard Chapman relating
  to Terhune's newspaper articles.

  papers, 1890-1941. 7 ft. ca. 580 items
  In Library of Congress, Manuscript Division (Washington,
  D.C.)
  Correspondence, documents, literary mss., articles,
  addresses, and radio scripts. Includes typewritten copies of
  4 articles by John T. Scarry, a biographical sketch of
  Terhune by John F. Trow, Jr. and a manuscript and typescript
  of THE BURT TERHUNE I KNEW (1943), by Anice Terhune.

TEXT-BOOK ASSOCIATION OF PHILADELPHIA
  records, 1866-96. ca. 150 items
  In Haverford College Library, Quaker Collection (Haverford,
  Pa.)
  Correspondence and other records of an organization which
  sponsored the writing and publishing of school histories
  compatible with the principles of the Society of Friends.
  Includes papers relating to the formation of the association

TEXT-BOOK ASSOCIATION OF PHILADELPHIA
(1866); letters from prospective authors (1866-69);
copyrights, agreements and correspondence (1889-96) with
Allen Clapp Thomas (1846-1920); correspondence and
agreements (1881-85) with Sydney Howard Gay (1814-88) and
Edward A. Thomas concerning mss.; treasurer's account
book, receipts, and miscellaneous correspondence.

THOMAS, ISAIAH, 1749-1831 (publisher)
papers, 1754-1831. 28 v. and 7 boxes
In American Antiquarian Society (Worcester, Mass.)
Letters, diaries, accounts, mss. of Thomas' HISTORY OF
PRINTING (1810); catalog of his books and other papers.

misc. papers, 1780-99. 48 items
In New York Historical Society (N.Y.)
Letters to Hudson and Goodwin, printers.(Hartford, Conn.)

THURBER, JAMES, 1894-1961 (A,I)
papers
In Ohio State Univ. Library (Columbus, Ohio)
Included in the collection are mss. of many of his books
and photographs.

TOLKIEN, J.R.R., 1892-1973 (A)
misc. papers
In Wheaton College Library (Wheaton, Ill.)
Includes notebooks, diaries, mss., and letters.

TROWBRIDGE, JOHN TOWNSEND, 1827-1916 (A)
papers, 1853-1906. 15 items and 21 v.
In Boston Public Library (Boston, Mass.)
Editor of OUR YOUNG FOLKS. Chiefly diaries and notebooks,
together with 15 letters from Trowbridge relating to his
work.

misc. papers
In Johns Hopkins Univ. Library (Baltimore, Md.)

TROYER, JOHANNES, 1902-   (I)
original art. 20 items
In Emporia State Univ. Library, May Massee Collection
(Emporia, Kan.)
Misc. artwork for: THE ROMANCE OF WEIGHTS AND MEASURES (1960).

TUNIS, EDWIN, 1897-1973 (A,I)*
papers, 1951-73. 28 ft.
In Univ. of Oregon Library (Eugene, Or.)
Mss. and related material, original art work and professional
correspondence, mainly with Curtis Brown Ltd., and World

TUNIS, EDWIN
  Publishing Co.

TURNGREN, ANNETTE, 1902-   (A)
  misc. papers. 1.5 ft.
  In Univ. of Oregon Library (Eugene, Or.)
  Manuscript of one book as well as copies of her published
  work.

TWAIN, MARK
  pseud. see CLEMENS, SAMUEL LANGHORNE

UCHIDA, YOSHIKO, 1921-   (A)*
  papers, 1949-77. 6 boxes
  In Univ. of Oregon Library (Eugene, Or.)
  Correspondence with Harcourt, Brace, and Co., and Charles
  Scribner's Sons; literary mss., and galley proofs.

UNGERER, TOMI, 1931-   (A,I)*
  misc. papers, 1957-73. 599 items
  In Free Library of Philadelphia (Philadelphia, Pa.)
  Various materials including artwork, dummies, notes for the
  following titles: THE MELLOPS GO DIVING FOR TREASURE (1957),
  THE MELLOPS GO FLYING (1957), CRICTOR (1958), THE MELLOPS
  STRIKE OIL (1958), ADELAIDE (1959), CHRISTMAS EVE AT THE
  MELLOPS (1960), EMILE (1960), RUFUS (1961), SNAIL, WHERE ARE
  YOU? (1962), THE THREE ROBBERS (1962), COME INTO MY PARLOR
  (1963), THE MELLOPS GO SPELUNKING (1963), THE CLAMBAKE
  MUTINY (1964), FLAT STANLEY (1964), ONE, TWO WHERE'S MY SHOE?
  (1964), SELECTIONS FROM FRENCH POETRY (1965), MR. TALL AND
  MR. SMALL (1966), OH, WHAT NONESENSE! (1966), ORLANDO THE
  BRAVE VULTURE (1966), WARWICK'S THREE BOTTLES (1966), A CASE
  OF THE GIGGLES (1967), ZERALDA'S OGRE (1967), WHAT'S GOOD
  FOR A FOUR-YEAR-OLD? (1967), ASK ME A QUESTION (1968),
  LIMERICK GIGGLES, JOKE GIGGLES (1969), THE BOOK OF GIGGLES
  (1970), THE DONKEY RIDE (1973); collection also includes
  the following unpublished mss: ALFARO THE WHEELED PIRATE
  (manuscript became THE THREE ROBBERS), SONNTAG DER
  SAUFAMILIE SCHMUTZ, GUNDOLF THE HEARTLESS BOY, MAC DER
  RIESENHUND, THE MELLOPS AGAINST THE KIDNAPPERS, THE MELLOPS
  GOT A CAR; includes 3 series of drawings: PIG'S ART, PRATT
  RATSBY and TODDY TADDLE TAIL.

UNTERMEYER, LOUIS, 1885-1976 (editor)
  misc. papers, 1901-59. ca. "1,036 items"
  In Indiana Univ., Lilly Library (Bloomington, Ind.)

  misc. papers, 1906-40. 4 ft. 1,194 items
  In Univ. of Delaware Library (Newark, Del.)
  Letters (chiefly 1912-25) to Untermeyer from American and

UNTERMEYER, LOUIS
  British authors, editors and publishers, relating to
  various aspects of their literary activities; mss., and
  proofs of Untermeyer's MODERN AMERICAN POETRY (1919), MODERN
  BRITISH POETRY (1920), A TREASURY OF GREAT POEMS, ENGLISH AND
  AMERICAN (1942), THE WORLD'S WORST POETRY, and other
  writings. Correspondents include Leonie Adams, Conrad Aiken,
  William R. Benet, Maxwell Bodenheim, William S. B. Braith-
  waite, Witter Bynner, James B. Cabell, Nathalia Crane, Floyd
  Dell, Max Eastman, John G. Fletcher, Louis Golding, Eugene
  Jolas, Alfred Kreymborg, Walter Lippmann, Harriet Monroe,
  Merrill Moore, Gorham B. Munson, John Neihardt, Ezra Pound,
  John C. Ransom, Edwin A. Robinson, Muriel Rukeyser, Carl
  Sandburg, Siegfried Sassoon, Allen Tate, John H. Wheelock,
  Harry L. Wilson, Humbert Wolfe, and Clement Wood.

  THE UNTERMEYER-FROST COLLECTION
  misc. papers, 1915-63. 3 ft. 425 items
  In Library of Congress, Manuscript Division (Washington,
  D.C.)
  Letters (1915-58) from Robert Frost (1874-1963) to Untermeyer
  dealing with poets and poetry, religion, politics, Frost's
  philosophy, and other interests of the 2 men; poetry,
  articles, pamphlets, and books of Frost's work and autographed
  photos; together with correspondence, clippings, and other
  printed matter concerning Frost, collected by Untermeyer, and
  drafts and galley proofs of THE LETTERS OF ROBERT FROST TO
  LOUIS UNTERMEYER (1963).

UNWIN, NORA SPICER, 1907-   (A,I)*
  misc. papers, 1943-47. 4 ft.
  In Univ. of Oregon Library (Eugene, Or.)
  Original illustrations and proofs for MOUNTAIN BORN (1943),
  and original wood engraving, with print, of the blue-winged
  teal, for FOOTNOTES ON NATURE (1947).

VAN BUREN, RAEBURN, 1891-   (I)
  original art, 1951-66. 332 items
  In Boston Univ. Library, Department of Special
  Collections (Boston, Mass.)
  Original pen and ink drawings of the syndicated comic strip,
  "Abbie and Slats;" charcoal drawings for SATURDAY EVENING
  POST; miscellaneous pencil and charcoal drawings.

VAN LOON, HENDRIK WILLEM, 1882-1944 (A,I)*
  misc. papers. 1 item
  In Free Library of Philadelphia (Philadelphia, Pa.)
  Typescript and illustrations for HISTORY OF AMERICA FROM THE
  DISCOVERY TO THE EARLIEST SETTLEMENT.

VAN STOCKUM, HILDA, 1908-   (A,I)*
original art. 74 items
In Emporia State Univ. Library, May Massee Collection
(Emporia, Kan.)
Misc. artwork for: THE MITCHELLS (1945), THE ANGELS'
ALPHABET (1948), CANADIAN SUMMER (1948).

VILLAREGO, MARY (I)
original art. 27 items
In Emporia State Univ. Library, May Massee Collection
(Emporia, Kan.)
Misc. artwork for: A SANTO FOR PASQUALITA (1959).

WAITE, ESTHER (A,I)
original art. 43 items
In Emporia State Univ. Library, May Massee Collection
(Emporia, Kan.)
Misc. artwork for: KATE FARLEY, PIONEER (1939), SUSAN (1944).

WALKER, MORT, 1923-   (I)
original art, 1955-66. 350 items
In Boston Univ. Library, Department of Special
Collections (Boston, Mass.)
Original pen and ink drawings of the syndicated comic strip,
"Beetle Bailey."

WALLOWER, LUCILLE, 1910-   (A,I)
misc. papers, 1940. 38 items
In Free Library of Philadelphia (Philadelphia, Pa.)
Two typescripts of A CONCH SHELL FOR MOLLY (1940), original
lithographs, notes on canals.

WARD, LYND KENDALL, 1905-   (A,I)*
original art. 34 items
In Emporia State Univ. Library, May Massee Collection
(Emporia, Kan.)
Misc. artwork for: THE GOLDEN FLASH (1947), MANY MANSIONS
(1947), UP A CROOKED RIVER (1952), SANTIAGO (1955).

misc. papers, original art, 1951-62. 1 box
In Univ. of Oregon Library (Eugene, Or.)

WATSON, JANE WERNER, 1915-   (A)
papers, 1958-74. 3 ft., including 500 letters
In Univ. of Oregon Library (Eugene, Or.)
Papers include extensive correspondence with Artists and
Writers Press, Inc., Golden Press, and Western Publishing Co.
There is also correspondence with Dr. Robert E. Switzer of the
Menninger Clinic regarding the writing of the Learning to
Know Yourself Series, a group of Golden Press books designed

WATSON, JANE WERNER
  to immunize the young against normal anxieties through the
  application of tot-psychology. Mss. of this series are
  also in the collection.

WEIL, LISL, 1910-   (A,I)*
  misc. papers and original art, 1967-75. 2 ft.
  In Univ. of Oregon Library (Eugene, Or.)
  Collection includes drafts, dummies, proofs, and related
  material.

WELLS, RHEA (A,I)
  original art. 114 items
  In Emporia State Univ. Library, May Massee Collection
  (Emporia, Kan.)
  Misc. artwork for: PEPPI THE DUCK (1927), AN AMERICAN FARM
  (1928), COCO THE GOAT (1929), OLD TALES FROM SPAIN (1929),
  BEPPO THE DONKEY (1930), ALI THE CAMEL (1931), ANDY AND
  POLLY (1932), ZEKE THE RACOON (1933).

WERNER, VIVIAN LESCHER (A)
  papers, 1961-71. 3 ft.
  In Univ. of Oregon Library (Eugene, Or.)
  Papers consist of mss. in various stages, source material, and
  correspondence. Major correspondence is with agents Rosica
  Colin and Lenniger Literary Agency, and with publishers
  Macmillan, Rupert Hart-Davis, and Doubleday.

WERTH, KURT, 1896-   (I)*
  papers and original art, 1930-77. 1,200 pieces
  In Univ. of Oregon Library (Eugene, Or.)
  Includes mss., sketches, rough layouts, dummies, and
  finished artwork for books; cartoons and sketches from early
  career in Germany before World War II.

WHITE, ANNE TERRY, 1896-   (A)
  misc. papers, 1963-68. ca. 2 ft.
  In Univ. of Oregon Library (Eugene, Or.)
  Mss. of original works and translations from the Russian;
  together with correspondence with publishers, especially
  George Braziller, Thomas Y. Crowell, and Garrard Publishers.

WHITE, E. B., 1899-   (A)
  misc. papers and photographs
  In Cornell Univ., John M. Olin Library (Ithaca, N.Y.)

WIESE, KURT, 1887-1974 (A,I)*
  original art. 1 item
  In Emporia State Univ. Library, May Massee Collection

WIESE, KURT
  (Emporia, Kan.)
  Misc. artwork for: THE ROUND MEADOW (1951).

  original art, 1930-70. 15 ft.
  In Univ. of Oregon Library (Eugene, Or.)
  Original illustrations and related material for 65 books.

WILDER, LAURA INGALLS, 1867-1957 (A)
  misc. papers
  In Pomona Public Library (Pomona, Calif.)
  Collection consists of 22 autograph letters; 2 letters to LIW;
  37 letters about the author; 8 autograph letters from Rose
  Wilder Lane; 2 letters to RWL; holograph manuscript of LITTLE
  HOUSE ON THE PRAIRIE (1935); typescripts of THE SHORES OF
  SILVER LAKE (1939) and WEST FROM HOME (1974); 116 photographs
  and miscellaneous material.

WILLIAMS, BERKELEY (I)*
  original art. 10 items
  In Emporia State Univ. Library, May Massee Collection
  (Emporia, Kan.)
  Misc. artwork for: BARRIE AND DAUGHTER (1943).

WILLIS, NATHANIEL PARKER, 1806-1867 (poet)
  misc. papers, 1832-65. 87 items
  In Detroit Public Library, Burton Historical Collection
  (Detroit, Mich.)
  Correspondence relating to personal affairs and literary
  interest of Willis and his colleagues, including
  correspondence with Brantz Mayer concerning publication of
  Mayer's MEXICO AS IT WAS AND AS IT IS(1844) and his career
  in the diplomatic service.

WILSON, CHARLES MORROW, 1905-1977 (A)
  papers, 1928-74. 8 ft.
  In Univ. of Oregon Library (Eugene, Or.)
  Papers consist of personal and professional correspondence,
  and published pieces. Major correspondents include
  Auerbach, Doubleday, Univ. of Florida Press, Funk and Wagnalls,
  Hastings House, Holt, Rinehart and Winston, P.J. Kenedy,
  Macmillan, Macrae-Smith, David McKay, Oklahoma Univ. Press,
  Stackpole, and Van Nostrand. Editorial correspondence is
  with Harper's, Reader's Digest and Vermont Life.

WILSON, EDWARD ARTHUR, 1886-1970 (I)
  papers, 1911-62. 23 ft.
  In Univ. of Oregon Library (Eugene, Or.)
  Papers consist of original artwork, proofs and allied material
  for book illustrations. Correspondents include Doubleday,

WILSON, EDWARD ARTHUR
George Macy and Frank Shay.

WOOLLEY, CATHERINE, 1904-   (A)
misc. papers, 1940-69. ca. 2 ft.
In Univ. of Oregon Library (Eugene, Or.)
Correspondence with publishers, especially William Morrow.

WYCHE STORY LEAGUE
records, 1934-61. 1 ft.
In Tacoma Public Library (Tacoma, Wash.)
Minutes, scrapbooks, programs, and membership lists of the
Des Moines, Wash. branch of the National Story League, an
organization interested in stories and storytelling.

WYETH, NEWELL CONVERS, 1882-1945 (I)
misc. family papers, 1880-1929. 80 items
In Boston Public Library (Boston, Mass.)
Correspondence to and from members of the Wyeth family,
together with some photos of Wyeth's children.

misc. papers. original art
In Free Library of Philadelphia, Thornton Oakley Collection
(Philadelphia, Pa.)

original art. 26 items
In Reference Library, Ginn and Co. (Lexington, Mass.)
Library holds 26 original paintings for "The World of Music
Series" edited by Mabelle Glenn and Helen S. Levitt.

original art. 10 items
In Needham Free Public Library (Needham, Mass.)
The 10 paintings held by the Library are described in "Some
Notes on the N.C. Wyeth Collection" published by the library.

WYNDHAM, LEE
pseud. see HYNDMAN, JANE ANDREWS

YATES, ELIZABETH, 1905-   (A)*
papers, 1927-65. 5 ft.
In Boston Univ. Library (Boston, Mass.)
Correspondence, literary mss., research notes, publicity
material, photos, reviews, and memorabilia. Includes material
on Rev. Howard Thurman, assembled for Miss Yates' biography
of him.

misc. papers, photographs
In Emporia State Univ. Library, May Massee Collection
(Emporia, Kan.)

YAUKEY, GRACE SYDENSTRICKER, 1899-   (A)
  misc. papers, 1934-66. 3 ft.
  In Univ. of Oregon Library (Eugene, Or.)
  Correspondence with publishers and mss. of books and articles.

YOUNG FEMALE RELIGIOUS TRACT SOCIETY
  WILLIAM ELMER, b. 1814 (physician)
  papers, 1808-79. 2 boxes
  In Rutgers Univ. Library (New Brunswick, N.J.)
  Bills and receipts for personal expenditures; accounts and
  lists of bonds and notes held; constitution and accounts of
  the Young Female Religious Tract Society of Bridgeton, and
  other papers.

ZIM, HERBERT SPENCER, 1909-   (A)*
  papers, 1934-75. 42 ft.
  In Univ. of Oregon Library (Eugene, Or.)
  Mss. of writings, artwork, correspondence (1952-60) with
  Spencer Press, correspondence (1959-67) with Golden Press,
  and published works.

ADDENDA

ANDREWS, SIRI MARGRETA, 1894-1973 (librarian)
  misc. papers
  In New Hampshire State Library (Concord, N.H.)
  Collection contains miscellaneous mss. of lectures given
  by Miss Andrews.

BURGESS, THORNTON W., 1874-1965 (A)
  misc. papers
  In Thornton W. Burgess Society Library (Sandwich, Mass.)
  Includes correspondence, photos., memorabilia and clipping
  file.

KEATS, EZRA JACK, 1916-   (A,I)*
  papers, original art. ca. 500 items
  In Harvard Univ., Gutman Library (Cambridge, Mass.)
  Collection contains original artwork, mss. of books, galley
  proofs, correspondence and other records relating to his
  career. Collection is partially cataloged.

LEIGHTON, JOHN, 1822-1912 (I)
  original art
  In Providence Public Library (Providence, R.I.)
  12 original drawings for THE DIVERTING HISTORY OF JOHN
  GILPIN (1845), by William Cowper.

MCCAY, WINSOR, 1869-1934 (I)
  misc. original art. ca. 80 items
  In Fairleigh Dickinson Univ., Friendship Library, Harry A.
  Chesler Collection (Madison, N.J.)

TITLE INDEX

The following title index includes the author's name in parenthesis:

Bright April (DE ANGELI, MARGUERITE) 24
Bronze Bow (SPEARE, ELIZABETH) 69
Buffalo Bill (AULAIRE, EDGAR P. D') 8
Burt Dow (MCCLOSKEY, ROBERT) 52
C. is for Cupcake (HAYWOOD, CAROLYN) 39
Caddie Woodlawn (BRINK, CAROL) 66
Calico Captive (SPEARE, ELIZABETH) 69
Calico, the Wonder Horse (BURTON, VIRGINIA) 14
Canadian Summer (VAN STOCKUM, HILDA) 78
Candy Floss (GODDEN, RUMER) 3
Candy Stripers (HYNDMAN, JANE) 42
Captain Kidd's Cat (LAWSON, ROBERT) 47
Carry On, Mr. Bowditch (LATHAM, JEAN) 47
Case of the Giggles (UNGERER, TOMI) 76
Castle Number Nine (BEMELMANS, LUDWIG) 11
Cat That Walked a Week (DE JONG, MEINDERT) 25
Celebrity at Home (KIPLING, RUDYARD) 45
Centerburg Tales (MCCLOSKEY, ROBERT) 52
Chestry Oak (SEREDY, KATE) 66
Child of Calamity (KIPLING, RUDYARD) 45
Children of the Covered Wagon (CARR, MARY JANE) 15
Chinese Ginger Jars (SCOVEL, MYRA) 66
Christ Child (PETERSHAM, MAUD / PETERSHAM, MISKA) 59
Christmas Eve at the Mellops (UNGERER, TOMI) 76
Chuggy and the Blue Caboose (FREEMAN, LYDIA / FREEMAN, DON) 33
Circle of Quiet (L'ENGLE, MADELEINE) 48
Clambake Munity (UNGERER, TOMI) 76
Coal Camp Girl (LENSKI, LOIS) 49
Coco the Goat (WELLS, RHEA) 79
Come Again, Pelican (FREEMAN, DON) 33
Come Into My Parlour (UNGERER, TOMI) 76
Conch Shell for Mollie (WALLOWER, LUCILLE) 78
Corn Farm Boy (LENSKI, LOIS) 49
Corn Grows Ripe (RHOADS, DOROTHY) 16
Corporal Keeperupper (MILHOUS, KATHERINE) 55
Country Colic (LAWSON, ROBERT) 47
Country-Stop (BAILEY, CAROLYN) 59
Crictor (UNGERER, TOMI) 76
Crock of Gold (STEPHENS, JAMES) 47
Cruise of the Arctic Star (O'DELL, SCOTT) 58
Daniel Boone (DAUGHERTY, JAMES) 24
Daniel Boone (WHITE, STEWART EDWARD) 24
Day's Work (KIPLING, RUDYARD) 45
Deepening Year (ROBINSON, MABEL) 64
Dexter (BULLA, CLYDE) 13
Dick Whittington & His Cat (LAWSON, ROBERT) 47
Dirk's Dog Bello (DE JONG, MEINDERT) 25
Disappearance of Anne Shaw (SEAMAN, AUGUSTA) 48
Dog Next Door (ROBERTSON, KEITH) 25
Dog that Could Swim Under Water (THOMPSON, GEORGE) 26

Donkey Ride (UNGERER, TOMI) 76
Down Ryton Water (GAGGIN, EVA ROE) 36
Dragons in the Water (L'ENGLE, MADELEINE) 48
Drums of Monmouth (STERNE, EMMA) 47
Dutch Twins (PERKINS, LUCY) 59
Ear for Uncle Emil (GAGGIN, EVA ROE) 66
Echoes from the Sabine Farm (FIELD, EUGENE) 31
Eddie the Dog Holder (HAYWOOD, CAROLYN) 39
Edward, Hoppy and Joe (LAWSON, ROBERT) 47
Elephant and the Lark's Nest (KIPLING, RUDYARD) 45
Elin's Amerika (DE ANGELI, MARGUERITE) 24
Emile (UNGERER, TOMI) 76
Fabulous Flight (LAWSON, ROBERT) 47
Fairy Alphabet (MACKINSTRY, ELIZABETH) 53
Fairy Doll (GODDEN, RUMER) 3
Felita (KAHMANN, MABLE) 48
Fiddlestrings (DE ANGELI, MARGUERITE) 25
Fifty-four Forty or Fight! (CASTOR, HENRY) 16
Finders Keepers (RICHARDSON, MYRA REED) 33
Finnegan II (Bailey, Carolyn) 66
Fire in the Wind (BROOKS, ANNE) 13
First Book of Ethiopia (STRONG, BARBARA) 73
First Book of the California Gold Rush (HAVIGHURST, WALTER) 70
First 3000 Years (FALLS, CHARLES) 30
Flat Stanley (UNGERER, TOMI) 30
Flight Today and Tomorrow (HYDE, MARGARET) 42
Fly High, Fly Low (FREEMAN, DON) 33
Flying Locomotive (DU BOIS, WILLIAM PÈNE) 28
For the Leg of a Chicken (EHRLICH, BETTINA) 29
Four & Twenty Blackbirds (FISH, HELEN) 47
From Sea to Sea (KIPLING, RUDYARD) 45
From the Horn of the Moon (MASON, ARTHUR) 47
Gaily We Parade (BREWTON, JOHN) 47
Galileo and the Magic Numbers (ROSEN, SIDNEY) 70
Gentle Ben (MOREY, WALTER) 56
Get-a-way and Háry János (PETERSHAM, MAUD / PETERSHAM, MISKA) 60
Gilded Age (CLEMENS, SAMUEL) 19
Golden Flash (MCNEER, MAY) 78
Golden Fleece (CALL, HUGHIE) 14
Golden Horseshoe (COATSWORTH, ELIZABETH) 47
Gold Luck Duck (DE JONG, MEINDERT) 25
Good Master (SEREDY, KATE) 66
Goose Girl (DE ANGELI, MARGUERITE) 25
Gray Caps (KNOX, ROSE) 48
Great Dane Thor (FARLEY, WALTER) 30
Great-Grandfather in the Honey Tree (SWAYNE, SAMUEL) 73
Great Lakes Sailor (RIETVELD, JANE) 63
Great Wheel (LAWSON, ROBERT) 47
Greylock and the Robins (ROBINSON, TOM) 47
Gundolf the Heartless Boy (UNGERER, TOMI) 76

Mr. T. W. Anthony Woo (ETS, MARIE HALL) 29
Mr. Tall and Mr. Small (UNGERER, TOMI) 76
Mr. Twigg's Mistake (LAWSON, ROBERT) 47
Mr. Wilmer (LAWSON, ROBERT) 47
Mrs. 'Arris Goes to Paris (GALLICO, PAUL) 34
Mrs. Bathurst (KIPLING, RUDYARD) 45
Mitchells (VAN STOCKUM, HILDA) 78
Monkey Island (RIETVELD, JANE) 63
Monkey Tale (WILLIAMSON, HAMILTON) 36
Moon Singer (BULLA, CLYDE) 13
Mop Top (FREEMAN, DON) 33
Mushroom Boy (HARPER, THEODORE ACLAND) 38
Mystery in the Square Tower (HONNESS, ELIZABETH) 41
Mystery of the Pirate's Ghost (HONNESS, ELIZABETH) 41
Mystery of the Secret Message (HONNESS, ELIZABETH) 41
Nicest Time of the Year (GAY, ZHENYA) 35
Nicholas and the Golden Goose (MOORE, ANNE) 55
Nicky's Bugle (RIETVELD, JANE) 63
Night of Power (KIPLING, RUDYARD) 45
Night the Lights Went Out (FREEMAN, DON) 33
Nikos and the Sea God (GRAMATKY, HARDIE) 35
Nine Days to Christmas (ETS, MARIE HALL / LABASTIDA, AURORA) 29
Nino (ANGELO, VALENTI) 7
Norman the Doorman (FREEMAN, DON) 33
Not One More Day (HILL, DONNA MARIE) 40
Oh, What Nonesense! (UNGERER, TOMI) 76
Old Curiosity Shop (DICKENS, CHARLES) 26
Old Jules (SANDOZ, MARI) 65
Old Tales from Spain (ALFAU, FELIPE) 79
Old Testament (DE ANGELI, MARGUERITE) 25
Once Upon a Time (MILHOUS, KATHERINE) 55
One Foot in Fairyland (FARJEON, ELEANOR) 47
One Morning in Maine (MCCLOSKEY, ROBERT) 52
One, Two Where's My Shoe (UNGERER, TOMI) 76
Open Gate (SEREDY, KATE) 66
Orlando the Brave Vulture (UNGERER, TOMI) 76
Pancakes for Breakfast (PAULL, GRACE) 59
Pancakes-Paris (BISHOP, CLAIRE) 65
Paradise (FORBES, ESTHER) 33
Peik (RING, BARBARA) 47
Peppi the Duck (WELLS, RHEA) 79
Philomena (SEREDY, KATE) 66
Pickwick (DICKENS, CHARLES) 27
Picnic (DAUGHERTY, JAMES) 24
Pilgram's Progress (BUNYAN, JOHN) 47
Pioneer Art in America (BAILEY, CAROLYN) 59
Poems for Children (DE LA MARE, WALTER) 25
Poo-Poo and the Dragons (FORESTER, CECIL) 47
Poppy Seed Cakes (CLARK, MARY / QUIGLEY, MARGERY) 59
Poseidon Adventure (GALLICO, PAUL) 34

KERLAN COLLECTION
HOLDINGS

Illustrators and Authors represented in the Kerlan Collection:

Aardema, Verna
Abbe, Elfriede Martha
Abisch, Roz
Adams, Adrienne
Adler, Irving
Adler, Peggy
Adler, Ruth
Alcock, Gudrun
Alcorn, John
Alger, Leclaire
Allen, Agnes
Allen, LeRoy
Altman, Elaine Joan
Ambrus, Victor G.
Ames, Lee J.
Amorosi, Nicholas
Amoss, Berthe
Anckarsvärd, Karin
Anderson, Clarence William
Anderson, John Lonzo
Angelo, Valenti
Anno, Mitsumasa
Ardizzone, Edward
Arkin, Alan
Armstrong, Gerry
Armstrong, William Howard
Arno, Enrico
Arnold, Pauline
Artzybasheff, Boris
Arundel, Jocelyn
Atwood, Ann
Auerbach, Marjorie
Aulaire, Edgar Parin d'
Aulaire, Ingri (Mortenson) d'
Averill, Esther Holden
Ayars, James Sterling
Ayer, Jacqueline
Ayer, Margaret
Bacon, Paul
Bacon, Peggy
Baker, Betty
Baker, Charlotte
Baker, Laura Nelson
Baldridge, Cyrus LeRoy
Bare, Arnold Edwin
Barker, Will
Barnes, Catherine

Barnouw, Victor
Barnstone, Aliki
Baron, Virginia Olsen
Barron, John N.
Barry, Katharina
Barry, Rogert E.
Barss, Bill
Barton, Byron
Batherman, Muriel
Bayer, Marion Dane
Bawden, Edward
Bayne, Stephen F.
Baynes, Pauline
Bealer, Alex W.
Bechtel, Louise (Seaman)
Behn, Harry
Bell, Anthea
Bell, Corydon
Bell, Thelma Harrington
Bellairs, John
Benary-Isbert, Margot
Bendick, Jeanne
Bennett, Richard
Berger, Terry
Bernard, Jacqueline
Berson, Harold
Berta, Hugh
Best, Allena (Champlin)
Beston, Henry
Bianco, Pamela
Bierhorst, John
Billings, Henry
Birch, Reginald Bathhurst
Blaisdell, Elinore
Bleeker, Sonia
Blegvad, Erik
Bleifeld, Stanley
Bloch, Lucienne
Bloch, Marie Halun
Blough, Glenn Orlando
Blume, Judy
Blust, Earl R.
Bock, Vera
Bødker, Arne
Bombová, Viera
Bonham, Frank
Bonsall, Crosby (Newell)

Booz, Elisabeth Benson
Borten, Helen
Bouchard, Lois Kalb
Bower, Louise
Boxer, Devorah
Bracker, Charles Eugene
Bradfield, Margaret
Brady, Lillian
Brandenberg, Aliki
Brandenburg, Franz
Branley, Franklyn Mansfield
Branscum, Robbie
Braun, Kathy
Braymer, Marjorie
Brenner, Barbara
Brink, Carol (Ryrie)
Brock, Emma Lillian
Broderick, Dorothy M.
Bronson, Wilfrid Swancourt
Brown, Judith Gwyn
Brown, Lloyd Arnold
Brown, Marcia
Brown, Margaret Wise
Brown, Palmer
Brown, Paul
Browning, Colleen
Brühl, Edelgard von Heydekampf
Brunhoff, Laurent de
Brustlein, Janice
Buckels, Alec
Buckley, Helen Elizabeth
Buff, Conrad
Bulla, Clyde Robert
Burger, Carl
Busch, Phyllis S.
Busoni, Rafaello
Butler, Francelia (McWilliams)
Byars, Betsy (Cromer)
Caines, Jeannette Franklin
Caldecott, Randolph
Calhoun, Mary
Cameron, Eleanor
Campbell, Virginia
Canfield, Jane White
Carle, Eric
Carlsen, Ruth Christoffer
Carlson, Natalie (Savage)
Carmer, Elizabeth (Black)
Carr, Mary Jane
Carrick, Carol

Carrick, Donald
Carter, Helene
Cassel-Wronker, Lili
Castagnetta, Grace
Caudill, Rebecca
Cavanah, Frances
Chafetz, Henry
Chalmers, Mary
Chandler, Edna Walker
Chapman, Frederick T.
Chappell, Warren
Charlip, Remy
Charlot, Jean
Chase, Richard
Chastain, Madye Lee
Chen, Tony
Cheney, Cora
Christgau, Alice E.
Chute, Beatrice Joy
Chute, Marchette Gaylord
Clark, Ann Nolan
Clarke, Arthur Charles
Cleary, Beverly
Cleaver, Bill
Cleaver, Vera
Coates, Belle
Coatsworth, Elizabeth Jane
Cober, Alan E.
Coen, Rena Neumann
Cohen, Miriam
Cohen, Robert Carl
Cohn, Angelo
Collins, Robert J.
Conford, Ellen
Connolly, Jerome P.
Cook, Howard Norton
Cooke, Donald Ewin
Cooley, Donald Gray
Coolidge, Olivia E.
Coombs, Patricia
Cooney, Barbara
Corbett, Scott
Corcoran, Barbara
Corcos, Lucille
Corey, Robert
Cornwall, Ian Wolfram
Cosgrave, John O'Hara II
Cosgrave, Margaret
Cowell, Vi
Cox, Palmer

Crawford, Mel
Crayder, Dorothy
Credle, Ellis
Creekmore, Raymond
Cretan, Gladys Yessayan
Cretien, Paul D.
Crews, Donald
Crowell, Ann
Crowell, Pers
Cruikshank, George
Cruse, Laurence
Cruz, Ray
Cuffari, Richard
Cullen, Charles
Cummings, Betty Sue
Cunningham, Julia
Dahl, Borghild Margarethe
Dalgliesh, Alice
Dalke, Susan Salladé
Daugherty, Harry
Daugherty, James Henry
Davis, Paul
Davis, Russell G.
De Angeli, Marguerite (Lofft)
De Jong, Meindert
De la Mare, Walter John
Delton, Judy
Dennis, Wesley
Denslow, William Wallace
De Paola, Thomas Anthony
De Pauw, Linda Grant
Detmold, Edward Julius
DeWitt, Cornelius Hugh
Dick, Trella Lamson
Dines, Glen
Disney (Walt) Productions
Divers, Dorothy
Doane, Pelagie
Domanska, Janina
Domjan, Joseph
Dorliae, Peter G.
Dowden, Anne Ophelia
Downer, Marion
Duffy, Joseph
Duncan, Lois
Duvoisin, Roger Antoine
Earle, Olive Lydia
Eaton, Jeanette
Eberle, Irmengarde
Ecke, Wolfgang

Edmonds, Walter Dumaux
Ehlert, Lois
Ehrlich, Bettina
Eichenberg, Fritz
Emberley, Ed
Emrich, Duncan
Erdoes, Richard
Erickson, Phoebe
Esbensen, Barbara Juster
Escourido, Joseph
Espenscheid, Gertrude Elliott
Estes, Eleanor
Ets, Marie Hall
Evans, Katherine
Eyerly, Jeannette
Faber, Doris
Farber, Norma
Farquhar, Margaret C.
Fast, Julius
Fatio, Louise
Faulknor, Cliff
Fax, Elton C.
Feague, Mildred H.
Feaser, Daniel D.
Fehrenbach, T.R.
Feil, Hila
Fenisong, Ruth
Fetz, Ingrid
Fiammenghi, Gioia
Fife, Dale
Fine, Aaron
Fischer, Hans
Fisher, Leonard Everett
Fitzgerald, John Dennis
Floethe, Louise Lee
Floethe, Richard
Flora, James
Forberg, Ati
Ford, Henry Justice
Foster, Genevieve (Stump)
Foster, Marian Curtis
Fox, Michael
Frame, Paul
Frankenberg, Robert C.
Frazier, Neta (Lohnes)
Freeman, Don
Freschet, Berniece
Freund, Rudolf
Fribourg, Marjorie G.
Fritz, Jean

Froman, Elizabeth Hull
Fuller, Catherine Leuthold
Funai Mamoru
Funk, Clotilde Embree
Gág, Flavia
Gág, Wanda
Galdone, Paul
Gannett, Ruth Crisman
Gates, Doris
Gay, Zhenya
Gehr, Mary
Geisel, Theodor Seuss
Gekiere, Madeleine
George, Jean Craighead
Gergely, Tibor
Giacoia, Frank
Gilchrist, Theo E.
Gillham, Charles Edward
Ginsburg, Mirra
Giovanopoulos, Paul
Gobbato, Imero
Godwin, Edward F.
Godwin, Stephani (Allfree)
Goff, Lloyd Lōzed
Goodenow, Earle
Goodman, Elaine
Goodman, Walter
Gordon, Ayala
Goudey, Alice E.
Graham, Lorenz B.
Graham, Margaret Bloy
Gramatky, Hardie
Granahan, David
Granahan, Lolita
Gray, Nigel
Green, Roger Lancelyn
Greenaway, Kate
Greenberg, Polly
Greene, Carla
Greer, Blanche
Gross, Ruth Belov
Guggenheim, Hans
Haas, Irene
Hader, Berta (Hoerner)
Hader, Elmer
Hale, Katheleen
Haley, Gail E.
Hall, Elvajean
Hall, Gordon Langley
    See also Simmons, Dawn Langley
Hall, Lynn

Hamilton, Katherine Parr
Hample, Stuart E.
Hamre, Leif
Handforth, Thomas
Hanson, Joan
Harvey, Lois F
Haugaard, Erick Christian
Havighurst, Marion M. (Boyd)
Havighurst, Walter
Hayes, Geoffrey
Haynes, Bob
Hays, Wilma Pitchford
Haywood, Carolyn
Heiderstadt, Dorothy
Hemphill, Josephine
Henry, Joanne Landers
Henry, Marguerite
Henstra, Friso
Hess, Lowell
Heyer, William
Hightower, Florence
Hill, Jeff
Hirawa, Yasuko
Hirsch, S. Carl
Hnizdovsky, Jacques
Hoban, Lillian
Hoban, Russell
Hobbs, Barbara
Hodges, Cyril Walter
Hodges, Margaret
Hoff, Sydney
Hoffine, Lyla
Hoffman, Rosekrans
Hofsinde, Robert
Hogan, Inez
Hogner, Nils
Holding, James
Holl, Adelaide
Holland, Isabelle
Holland, Janice
Holland, Marion
Holman, Felice
Holtan, Gene
Hoover, H. M.
Hoover, Helen
Hopkins, Lee Bennett
Hough, Richard Alexander
Houser, Lowell
Hull, Eleanor (Means)
Hummel, Arthur W.
Humphrey, Henry

Humphries, Stella
Hunt, Irene
Hunt, Mabel Leigh
Hunter, Ted, Mark & Richard
Hurd, Clement
Hurd, Edith (Thacher)
Hyman, Trina Schart
Ilsley, Velma
Ipcar, Dahlov (Zorach)
Irving, James Gordon
Ivan, Martha Miller (Pfaff)
Ivanowsky, Élizabeth
Jackson, Jacqueline
Jackson, Robert B.
Jacobs, Leslie
Jansons, Inese
Jaques, Florence (Page)
Jaques, Francis Lee
Jauss, Anne Marie
Jeffries, Roderic
Jemne, Elsa
Jenkyns, Chris
Jensen, Henning Black
Jensen, Virginia Allen
Johnson Annabell
Johnson, Edgar
Johnson, Elizabeth
Jones, Elizabeth Orton
Jones, Harold
Jones, Henrietta
Jones, Weyman B.
Jonk, Clarence
Judah, Aaron
Judson, Clara (Ingram)
Kahl, Ann
Kamen, Gloria
Kantrowitz, Mildred
Kaplan, Boche
Karl, Jean
Kashiwagi, Isami
Kavaler,Lucy
Kaye, Gertrude
Keats, Ezra Jack
Keeler, Katherine (Southwick)
Keeping, Charles
Kelsey, Vera
Kent, Jack
Kepes,Juliet
Kerr, M. E.
Kessler, Leonard P.

Kiddel-Monroe, Joan
King, Edna Knowles
King, Joseph T.
Kingman, Lee
Kingsland, L. W.
Kirk, Ruth
Kirn, Ann
Kismaric, Carole
Kissin, Eva H.
Kjelgaard, James Arthur
Klapholz, Mel
Klein, Norma
Krahn, Fernando
Kraner, Florian
Kraus, Robert
Kredel, Fritz
Kroll, Edite
Krush, Beth
Kuskin, Karla
Laklan, Carli
Lambo, Don
Lammers, Ann Conrad
Landau, Jacob
Langton, Jane
La Palme, Robert
Lasker, Joe
Latham, Barbara
Latham, Jean Lee
Lathrop, Dorothy Pulis
Lattimore, Eleanor Frances
Lawrence, James Duncan
Lawson, Marie (Abrams)
Lawson, Robert
Laycock, George
Lee, Doris (Emrick)
Lee, Manning de Villeneuve
Lee, Mildred
Le Gallienne, Eva
Leighton, Margaret (Carver)
Lemke, Horst
L'Engle, Madeleine
Lenski, Lois
Lerner, Sharon
Levitin, Sonia
Lewis, Allen
Lexau, Joan M.
Lindstrom, Sister Eleanor L.
Lipkind, William
Lipsyte, Robert
Little, Jean

Olds, Elizabeth
Olsen, Ib Spang
O'Neill, Mary (Le Duc)
Orgel, Doris
Palazzo, Tony
Panetta, George
Parish, Peggy
Parker, Edgar
Parker, John
Parks, Gordon
Parson, Ellen
Paterson, Katherine
Paull, Grace
Paw OO Thet, U.
Payne, Joan Balfour
Payson, Dale
Payzant, Charles
Peck, Richard
Peet, Bill
Perceval, Don
Petersham, Maud (Fuller)
Petersham, Miska
Peterson, Betty F.
Peterson, Harold Leslie
Petie, Harris
Pine, Tillie S.
Pitz, Henry Clarence
Piussi-Campbell, Judy
Plotz, Helen
Polgreen, John
Politi, Leo
Pope, Elizabeth Marie
Porter, Jean MacDonald
Potter, Beatrix
Potter, Bronson
Potter, Miriam (Clark)
Potter, Zenas
Powers, Richard M.
Preissler, Audrey
Prelutsky, Jack
Price, Christine
Price, Edith Ballinger
Price, Garrett W.
Pyk, Ann
Quackenbush, Robert M.
Quigley, Lillian Fox
Raskin, Ellen
Rasmussen, Halfdan Wedel
Ray, Deborah
Ray, Ralph, Jr.

Reed, Philip
Remington, Barbara
Ressner, Philip
Rey, Hans Augusto
Reyher, Rebecca (Hourwich)
Reynolds, Marjorie
Rhoads, Dorothy
Richardson, Grace Haddon
Rigolo, Stanislao Dino
Rinkoff, Barbara
Ripper, Charles L.
Rivoli, Mario
Robbins, Ruth
Robertson, Lilian
Robinson, Charles
Robinson, Irene Bowen
Robinson, Thomas Pendleton
Robinson, William Wilcox
Rocker, Fermin
Rockwell, Anne F.
Rockwell, Harlow
Rodgers, Mary
Rodman, Maia Wojciechowska
    See also Wojciechowska,
    Maia
Roetter, Sonia
Rojankovsky, Feodor
Rosenberg, Ethel (Clifford)
Rosier, Lydia
Rosselli, Colette
Rounds, Glen
Rouse, David
Rouse, Donald
Rowand, Phyllis
Rudolph, Marguerita
Russell, Solveig Paulson
Sachs, Marilyn
Sage, Michael
St. John, Wylly Folk
Salem, Mary Miller
Samson, Anne Stringer
Sandberg, Lasse
Sandin, Joan
Sauer, Julia Lina
Saviozzi, Adriana Mazza
Scarry, Richard
Schachner, Erwin
Schick, Eleanor
Schiller, Barbara
Schlein, Miriam

Schloat, G. Warren
Schmidt, Harvey
Scholberg, Genry
Schreiber, Georges
Scott, Alma Olivia (Schmidt)
Scott, Ann Herbert
Sears, Paul McCutcheon
Seiden, Art
Seignobosc, Françoise
Sendak, Jack
Sendak, Maurice
Seroff, Victor Ilyitch
Servello, Joe
Sewall, Marcia
Sewell, Helen
Shannon, Terry
Shaw, Evelyn S.
Shaw, Richard
Shecter, Ben
Shenton, Edward
Shepard, Ernest Howard
Shimin, Symeon
Shinn, Everett
Showalter, Jean B.
Showers, Paul
Shub, Elizabeth
Siberell, Anne
Sibley, Don
Sidjakov, Nicolas
Siebel, Fritz
Siegl, Helen
Silverman, Mel
Simmons, Dawn Langley
  See also Hall, Gordon Langley
Simon, Norma
Simont, Marc
Slobodkin, Louis
Slobodkina, Esphyr
Smith, Alvin
Smith, Glanville Wynkoop
Smith, Howard Jerome
Smith, Merrily A.
Smith, William Jay
Smucker, Barbara Claassen
Snyder, Zilpha Keatley
Sobol, Donald J.
Söderhjelm, Kai
Sokol, William
Solbert, Ronno
Sorel, Edward

Sorensen, Virginia E.
Sotomayor, Antonio
Sperry, Armstrong
Spier, Peter
Spilka, Arnold
Stahl, Benjamin Albert
Starkey, Marion Lena
Steele, Mary Q.
Steele, William O.
Steen, Vagn
Steichen, Edward
Steig, William
Stein, Harvé
Steiner, Charlotte
Stern, Madeleine Bettina
Stern, Marie (Simchow)
Steven, Leslie
Stinetorf, Louise A.
Stobbs, William
Stolz, Mary (Slattery)
Stone, Helen
Stoutenburg, Adrien
Stover, Jo Ann
Strachan, Margaret Pitcairn
Stubis, Tālivaldis
Stull, Betty
Suba, Susanne
Suckling, E. E.
Suggs, William W.
Sutcliff, Rosemary
Szekeres, Cyndy
Taback, Simms
Takakjian, Portia
Tanner, Louise (Stickney)
Tate, Joan
Taylor, Sydney
Taylor, Theodore
Tenggren, Gustaf
Thollander, Earl
Thomas, Jane Resh
Thompson, Mozelle
Tillett, Leslie
Tinkelman, Murray
Tippett, James Sterling
Tolford, Joshua
Tomes, Margot
Toschik, Larry
Townsend, John Rowe
Trease, Geoffrey
Trelease, Allen W.

Tresselt, Alvin R.
Tudor, Tasha
Tunis, Edwin
Turngren, Ellen
Uchida, Yoshiko
Ungerer, Tomi
Unwin, Nora Spicer
Uttley, Alison
Valens, Evans G.
Vance, Eleanor (Graham)
Van Loon, Hendrik Willem
Van Stockum, Hilda
Van Woerkom, Dorothy O.
Vasiliu, Mircea
Vaughan, Anne
Virost, Judith
Vizenor, Gerald Robert
Vogel, Ilse-Margret
Von Schmidt, Eric
Voss, Carroll
Voute, Kathleen
Waber, Bernard
Wagner, Jane
Wagner, Lauren McGraw
Wahl, Jan
Walker, Barbara K.
Walker, Charles
Ward, Lynd Kendall
Warner, Edythe Records
Wartik, Herschel
Watson, Aldren Auld
Weaver, Robert G.
Webber, Irma Eleanor (Schmidt)
Weik, Mary Hays
Weil, Lisl
Weisgard, Leonard
Weiss, Emil
Weiss, Harvey
Wellman, Alice
Wells, Luther Coleman
Werth, Kurt
Weygant, Noemi
White, Bessie (Felstiner)
White, David Omar
Whitney, Thomas P.
Wier, Ester
Wiese, Kurt
Wiesner, William
Wilcox, Eleanor Reindollar
Williams, Berkeley, Jr.

Williamson, Hamilton
Wilson, Dagmar
Wilson, Edward Arthur
Wilson, Hazel (Hutchins)
Wilwerding, Walter Joseph
Windsor, Patricia
Winsor, Robert
Winter, Ginny Linville
Winter, William
Winthrop, Elizabeth
Wise, William
Witheridge, Elizabeth P.
Wohlberg, Meg
Wojciechowska, Maia
  See also Rodman, Maia
  Wojciechowska
Wong, Jeanyee
Woods, George A.
Woodward, Hildegard
Worcester, Donald Emmet
Wrightson, Patricia
Yamaguchi, Marianne
Yashima, Tarō
Yates, Elizabeth
Yolen, Jane H.
Young, Ed
Zagoren, Ruby
Zallinger, Jean Day
Zehnpfennig, Gladys
Zemach, Harve
Zim, Herbert Spencer
Zion, Gene
Zolotow, Charlotte (Shapiro)

INSTITUTIONAL
DIRECTORY

The following is a directory of institutions cited in the text:

ADAMS COUNTY HISTORICAL SOCIETY LIBRARY
   Confederate Ave., Lutheran Theological Seminary Campus,
   Drawer A, Gettysburg, Pa. 17325

AMERICAN ACADEMY OF ARTS AND LETTERS LIBRARY
   633 W. 155th St., New York, N.Y. 10032

AMERICAN ANTIQUARIAN SOCIETY LIBRARY
   185 Salisbury St., Worcester, Mass. 01609

AMERICAN JEWISH ARCHIVES
   Cincinnati, Ohio 45202

AMERICAN MUSEUM OF NATURAL HISTORY LIBRARY
   79th St. and Central Park W., New York, N.Y. 10024

AMISTAD RESEARCH CENTER LIBRARY
   Dillard Univ., 2601 Gentilly Blvd., New Orleans, La. 70122

AMOS MEMORIAL LIBRARY
   230 E. North St., Sidney, Ohio 45365

ARCHIVES OF AMERICAN ART
   Smithsonian Institution, 41 E. 65th St., New York, N.Y. 10021

ARCHIVES OF EDGAR RICE BURROUGHS, INC.
   Tarzana, Calif.

ATLANTA UNIVERSITY
   Trevor Arnett Library, 273 Chestnut St. SW, Atlanta, Ga. 30314

BOSTON ATHENAEUM
   10 1/2 Beacon St., Boston, Mass. 02108

BOSTON PUBLIC LIBRARY
   666 Boylston St., Box 286, Boston, Mass. 02117

BOSTON UNIVERSITY
   Mugar Memorial Library, 771 Commonwealth Ave., Boston, Mass.
   02215

BOWDOIN COLLEGE LIBRARY
   Brunswick, Me. 04011

BUFFALO & ERIE COUNTY PUBLIC LIBRARY
   Lafayette Sq., Buffalo, N.Y. 14203

CAPITAL UNIVERSITY LIBRARY
2199 E. Main St., Columbus, Ohio 43209

CENTRAL CONNECTICUT STATE COLLEGE
Elihu Burritt Library, 1615 Stanley St., New Britain, Conn.
06050

CENTRAL MICHIGAN UNIVERSITY
Charles V. Park Library, Mount Pleasant, Mich. 48859

CLARK UNIVERSITY
Robert Hutchings Goddard Library, Worcester, Mass. 01610

COLBY COLLEGE
Miller Library, Waterville, Me. 04901

COLLEGE OF SAINTE CATHERINE
Sainte Catherine Library, 2004 Randolph Ave., Saint Paul,
Minn. 55105

COLLEGE OF WILLIAM AND MARY
Earl Gregg Swem Library, Williamsburg, Va. 23185

COLUMBIA UNIVERSITY
Butler Library, 535 W. 114th St., New York, N.Y. 10027

CONCORD FREE PUBLIC LIBRARY
129 Main St., Concord, Mass. 01742

CONNECTICUT COLLEGE LIBRARY
Mohegan Ave., New London, Conn. 06320

CONNECTICUT HISTORICAL SOCIETY LIBRARY
One Elizabeth St., Hartford, Conn. 06105

CORNELL UNIVERSITY LIBRARIES
Ithaca, N.Y. 14853

DEGOLYER LIBRARY
Southern Methodist Univ., Box 396, SMU Sta., Dallas, Tex.
75275

DELAWARE ART MUSEUM LIBRARY
2301 Kentmere Pkwy., Wilmington, Del. 19806

DENVER PUBLIC LIBRARY
1357 Broadway, Denver, Colo. 80203

DETROIT PUBLIC LIBRARY
5201 Woodward Ave., Detroit, Mich. 48202

DUKE UNIVERSITY
  William R. Perkins Library, Durham, N.C. 27706

EMPORIA STATE UNIVERSITY
  William Allen White Library, 1200 Commercial St.,
  Emporia, Kan. 66801

ERNEST THOMPSON SETON MEMORIAL LIBRARY
  Philmont Scout Ranch & Explorer Base, Cimarron, N.M. 87714

FAIRLEIGH DICKINSON UNIVERSITY
  Friendship Library, 285 Madison Ave., Madison, N.J. 07940

FISK UNIVERSITY LIBRARY AND MEDIA CENTER
  17th Ave. N., Nashville, Tenn. 37203

FLORIDA STATE UNIVERSITY
  Robert Manning Strozier Library, Tallahassee, Fla. 32306

FORBES LIBRARY
  20 West St., Northampton, Mass. 01060

FRANKLIN D. ROOSEVELT LIBRARY
  General Services Administration National Archives and
  Records Service, Hyde Park, N.Y. 12538

FREE LIBRARY OF PHILADELPHIA
  Logan Square, Philadelphia, Pa. 19103

GARDINER PUBLIC LIBRARY
  152 Water St., Gardiner, Me. 04345

HARTFORD PUBLIC LIBRARY
  500 Main St., Hartford, Conn. 06103

HARVARD UNIVERSITY
  Gutman Library, Houghton Library, Widener Library,
  Cambridge, Mass. 02138

HAVERFORD COLLEGE
  James P. Magill Library, Haverford, Pa. 19041

HENRY E. HUNTINGTON LIBRARY
  1151 Oxford Rd., San Marino, Calif. 91108

HISTORICAL SOCIETY OF PENNSYLVANIA LIBRARY
  1300 Locust St., Philadelphia, Pa. 19107

HOFSTRA UNIVERSITY LIBRARY
  1000 Fulton Ave., Hempstead, N.Y. 11550

ILLINOIS STATE UNIVERSITY LIBRARY
Normal, Ill. 61761

INDIANA UNIVERSITY
Lilly Library, Seventh St., Bloomington, Ind. 47401

INDIANAPOLIS-MARION COUNTY PUBLIC LIBRARY
40 E. St. Clair St., P.O. Box 211, Indianapolis, Ind. 46206

JOHNS HOPKINS UNIVERSITY
Milton S. Eisenhower Library, Baltimore, Md. 21218

JONES LIBRARY
43 Amity St., Amherst, Mass. 01002

KANSAS STATE HISTORICAL SOCIETY LIBRARY
120 W. Tenth, Topeka, Kan. 66612

LEHIGH UNIVERSITY
Linderman Memorial Library, Bethlehem, Pa. 18015

LIBRARY OF CONGRESS
Washington, D. C. 20540

MACCULLOCH HALL HISTORICAL MUSEUM
45 Macculloch Ave., Morristown, N.J. 07960

MCMASTER UNIVERSITY
Mills Memorial Library, 1280 Main St. W, Hamilton, Ontario
Canada L8S 4L6

MARK TWAIN BIRTHPLACE MEMORIAL SHRINE
Florida, Mo.

MARK TWAIN MEMORIAL
77 Forest St., Hartford, Conn. 06105

MASSACHUSETTS HISTORICAL SOCIETY LIBRARY
1154 Boylston St., Boston, Mass. 02215

METHODIST PUBLISHING HOUSE LIBRARY
Nashville, Tenn.

MILLICENT LIBRARY
Centre & William St., P.O. Box 30, Fairhaven, Mass. 02719

MISSOURI HISTORICAL SOCIETY LIBRARY
Jefferson Memorial Bldg., Saint Louis, Mo. 63122

MONTANA STATE UNIVERSITY LIBRARY
  Bozeman, Mont. 59717

NEBRASKA STATE HISTORICAL SOCIETY LIBRARY
  15 & R Sts., Lincoln, Neb. 68508

NEEDHAM FREE PUBLIC LIBRARY
  1139 Highland Ave., Needham, Mass. 02194

NEW HAMPSHIRE STATE LIBRARY
  20 Park St., Concord, N.H. 03301

NEW MEXICO STATE UNIVERSITY LBIRARY
  Box 3475, Las Cruces, N.M. 88003

NEW YORK HISTORICAL SOCIETY LIBRARY
  170 Central Park W., New York, N.Y. 10024

NEW YORK PUBLIC LIBRARY
  Fifth Ave. & 42nd St., New York, N.Y. 10018

NEW YORK STATE LIBRARY
  Cultural Education Center, Albany, N.Y. 12230

NEWBERRY LIBRARY
  60 W. Walton St., Chicago, Ill. 60610

NOOK FARM RESEARCH LIBRARY
  77 Forest St., Hartford, Conn. 06105

OAKLAND PUBLIC LIBRARY
  125 14th St., Oakland, Calif. 94712

OBERLIN COLLEGE ARCHIVES
  Seeley G. Mudd Learning Center, Oberlin, Ohio 44074

OHIO HISTORICAL SOCIETY LIBRARY
  I-71 & 17th Ave., Columbus, Ohio 43211

OHIO STATE UNIVERSITY LIBRARY
  1858 Neil Ave. Mall, Columbus, Ohio 43210

PHILIP H & A S W ROSENBACH FOUNDATION LIBRARY
  2010 DeLancey Pl., Philadelphia, Pa. 19103

PIERPONT MORGAN LIBRARY
  29 E. 36th St., New York, N.Y. 10016

POMONA PUBLIC LIBRARY
  Pomona, Calif.

PRESBYTERIAN HISTORICAL SOCIETY
425 Lombard, Philadelphia, Pa. 19103

PRINCETON UNIVERSITY LIBRARY
Nassau St., Princeton, N.J. 08540

PROVIDENCE PUBLIC LIBRARY
150 Empire St., Providence, R.I. 02903

PUBLIC LIBRARY OF CINCINNATI AND HAMILTON COUNTY
800 Vine St., Cincinnati, Ohio 45202

RADCLIFFE COLLEGE
Women's Archives, 3 James St., Cambridge, Mass. 02138

REFERENCE LIBRARY GINN AND COMPANY
191 Spring St., Lexington, Mass. 02173

RHODE ISLAND HISTORICAL SOCIETY LIBRARY
121 Hope St., Providence, R.I. 02906

RUTGERS UNIVERSITY LIBRARY
College Ave., New Brunswick, N.J. 08901

RUTHERFORD B. HAYES LIBRARY
1337 Hayes Ave., Fremont, Ohio 43420

SAINT JOHN'S SEMINARY
Edward Laurence Doheny Memorial Library, 5012 East Seminary
Rd., Camarillo, Calif. 93010

SAINT LAWRENCE UNIVERSITY
Owen D. Young Library, Park St., Canton, N.Y. 13617

SAN FRANCISCO PUBLIC LIBRARY
Civic Center, San Francisco, Calif. 94102

SANDWICH PUBLIC LIBRARY
Old Main St., Box 448, Sandwich, Mass. 02563

SILVERADO MUSEUM LIBRARY
1347 Railroad Ave. P.O. Box 409, Saint Helena, Calif. 94574

SMITH COLLEGE LIBRARY
Northampton, Mass. 01063

SOUTHERN ILLINOIS UNIVERSITY
Elijah P. Lovejoy Library, Edwardsville, Ill. 62025

STANFORD UNIVERSITY
University & Coordinate Libraries, Stanford, Calif. 94305

STATE HISTORICAL SOCIETY OF WISCONSIN LIBRARY
816 State St., Madison, Wisc. 53706

STATE UNIVERSITY NEW YORK COLLEGE AT BUFFALO
Edward H. Butler Library, 1300 Elmwood Ave., Buffalo, N.Y.
14222

STOWE-DAY MEMORIAL LIBRARY
77 Forest St., Hartford, Conn. 06105

SWARTHMORE COLLEGE
Friends Historical Library, Swarthmore, Pa. 19081

SYRACUSE UNIVERSITY LIBRARY
222 Waverly Ave., Syracuse, N.Y. 13210

TACOMA PUBLIC LIBRARY
1102 Tacoma Ave. S., Tacoma, Wash. 98402

TEMPLE UNIVERSITY LIBRARY
Berks & 13th Sts., Philadelphia, Pa. 19122

THORNTON W. BURGESS SOCIETY LIBRARY
Deacon House, Sandwich, Mass. 12563

TRINITY COLLEGE LIBRARY
300 Summit St., Hartford, Conn. 06106

UNIVERSITY OF ARKANSAS LIBRARIES
Fayetteville, Ark. 72701

UNIVERSITY OF CALIFORNIA, BERKELEY
Bancroft Library, Berkeley Calif. 94720

UNIVERSITY OF CALIFORNIA, DAVIS
General Library, Davis, Calif. 95616

UNIVERSITY OF CALIFORNIA, LOS ANGELES
405 Hilgard Ave., Los Angeles, Calif. 90024

UNIVERSITY OF CALIFORNIA, LOS ANGELES
William Andrews Clark Memorial Library, 2520 Cimarron St.,
Los Angeles, Calif. 90018

UNIVERSITY OF CHICAGO LIBRARY
1100 E. 57th St., Chicago, Ill. 60637

UNIVERSITY OF DELAWARE
Hugh M. Morris Library, Newark, Del. 19711

UNIVERSITY OF FLORIDA LIBRARIES
Gainesville, Fla. 32611

UNIVERSITY OF IOWA LIBRARIES
Iowa City, Iowa 52242

UNIVERSITY OF KANSAS
Kenneth Spencer Research Library, Lawrence, Kan. 066045

UNIVERSITY OF LOUISVILLE LIBRARY
2301 S. Third St., Louisville, Ky. 40208

UNIVERSITY OF MAINE AT ORONO
Raymond H. Fogler Library, Orono, Me. 04473

UNIVERSITY OF MICHIGAN
William L. Clements Library, Ann Arbor, Mich. 48104

UNIVERSITY OF NEBRASKA - LINCOLN
Don L. Love Memorial Library, Lincoln, Neb. 68588

UNIVERSITY OF NORTH CAROLINA - GREENSBORO
Walter Clinton Jackson Library, 1000 Spring Garden St.,
Greensboro, N.C. 27412

UNIVERSITY OF OKLAHOMA
William Bennett Bizzell Memorial Library, 401 W. Brooks,
Norman, Okla. 73019

UNIVERSITY OF OREGON LIBRARY
Eugene, Or. 97403

UNIVERSITY OF ROCHESTER
Rush Rhees Library, Rochester, N.Y. 14627

UNIVERSITY OF SOUTHERN MISSISSIPPI
Cook Memorial Library, Box 53, Southern Sta., Hattiesburg,
Miss. 39401

UNIVERSITY OF TEXAS AT AUSTIN
Humanities Research Center Library, Box P, Austin, Tex.
78712

UNIVERSITY OF VIRGINIA
Alderman Library, Charlottesville, Va. 22901

UNIVERSITY OF WASHINGTON LIBRARY
Seattle, Wash. 98195

UNIVERSITY OF WISCONSIN, MADISON
Memorial Library, 728 State St., Madison, Wisc. 53706

UNIVERSITY OF WYOMING
  William Robertson Coe Library, 13th & Ivinson, Laramie,
  Wyo. 82071

UTAH STATE UNIVERSITY
  Merrill Library & Learning Resources Program, Logan, Utah
  84322

WARDER PUBLIC LIBRARY
  Room 70, The Arcade, 137 E. High, Springfield, Ohio   45501

WASHINGTON STATE UNIVERSITY LIBRARY
  Pullman, Wash. 99163

WASHINGTON UNIVERSITY LIBRARY
  Skinner & Lindell Blvds., Saint Louis, Mo. 63130

WEST VIRGINIA UNIVERSITY LIBRARY
  Morgantown, W. Va. 26506

WESTBROOK COLLEGE LIBRARY
  716 Stevens Ave., Portland, Me.   04103

WESTERLY PUBLIC LIBRARY
  Broad St., Box 356, Westerly, R.I. 02891

WHEATON COLLEGE LIBRARY
  Irving & Franklin, Wheaton, Ill.   60187

YALE UNIVERSITY
  Beinecke Library, 120 High St., Box 1630A, Yale Sta.,
  New Haven, Conn. 06520